BASIC HOCKEY AND SKATING SKILLS

BASIC HOCKEY AND SKATING SKILLS

THE BACKYARD RINK APPROACH

JEREMY ROSE & MURRAY SMITH

POLESTAR

BOOK PUBLISHERS

Published by:
Polestar Press Ltd.
1011 Commercial Drive, Second Floor
Vancouver, BC
Canada   V5L 3X1
Write for a complete catalogue of our hockey titles.

Cover design and interior illustrations by Jim Brennan.
Cover photo by Bill Keay.
Interior photos by Joel Russ, Chris Relke and Bill Keay.
Bill Keay photos are copyright *Vancouver Sun*.
Printed in Canada by Best-Gagne Printers.
Produced by Kandace Kerr, Julian Ross and Michelle Benjamin.

All references to skates in this book are to hockey skates, not figure skates.

The skaters are not wearing helmets in the illustrations. However, as we have
emphasized in the text, we recommend that you wear a helmet at all times
while skating or playing hockey.

The publisher, Polestar Press Ltd., and the authors, Jeremy Rose and Murray
Smith, assume no responsibility for any injuries or accidents that may occur
while practicing the ice or in-line skating techniques described in this book.
Have fun and play safe.

Canadian Cataloguing in Publication Data
Rose, Jeremy M.C. (Jeremy Martin Cameron), 1958-
Basic hockey and skating skills
ISBN 0-919591-84-1
1. Hockey. 2. Skating. 3. In-line skating. 4. Skating rinks.
J. Smith, Murray, 1925 - Il. Title.
GV847.R68 1993   796.962   C93-091692-1

To the silent partners who have given support from the wings — friends and family in Canada and England too numerous to mention...you know who you are! Thanks especially to Leanne my wife for putting up with me during the final stages of the book, and to Murray for all his help and guidance...this was all his idea! Also regards to Tigger the cat who added some words of wisdom as he marched across the keyboard—what does jhi8ehv!* mean anyway?
—Jeremy Rose, October 1993

To Bob Raymond and his gravel truck. Bob coached the Edmonton Highlands Midgets and gave Breezy Dunsworth, Red Heron, me and a lot of other guys a great experience in a game we all loved. It helped convince me that a lifetime working with young people would be a good way to go. His open gravel truck took us on all of our "road" trips. The high box shielded us from the winter wind as well as from chunks of coal lobbed our way as we drove off after road games in Calder.
—Murray Smith, October 1993

The authors would like to thank the following staff and students of the Faculty of Physical Education and Recreation, University of Alberta, for their help and advice in preparing this manual: Audrey Bakewell, John Barry, Art Burgess, Clare Drake, Moira McPherson, Brian Nielsen and Dan Peacocke.

Also, a thank you to Ms. Anne Manwaring for her help in typing this manuscript, and Leanne Rose for her editorial comments. Thanks to Ian Pike for suggesting we publish this project, and to Wilf Brooks of United Cycle, Edmonton, for his tips about in-line skating. Finally, thanks to Les Thomas for doing the illustrations for our first draft.

The authors gratefully acknowledge the support of the Alberta Sport Council, who donated a research grant to aid in the preparation of an earlier version of this document.

LEGEND OF SYMBOLS 10

CHAPTER 1 / THE BACKYARD RINK APPROACH 11
Introduction 12
About This Book 14
How Children Develop Skills 15
The Learning Environment 16
The Importance of Practice and Skill Level 17
Fun and Play Keep Boredom Away! 17

CHAPTER 2 / EQUIPMENT 19
Children's Hockey Equipment 20
Ice Skates 20
Caring for Your Skates 21
Clothing 21
Helmet 21
The Stick 22
Homemade Alternatives to Regular Hockey Equipment ... 25

CHAPTER 3 / MAKING A HOMEMADE RINK 27
Location 28
Effects of Ice on Grass 28
Preparing the Site 29
The Size of the Rink 29
Types of Rink 30
The Bordered-Off Rink 30
    Materials 30
    Creating the Border 30
    Forming the Ice Surface 31
    Flooding 32
The Tank Method 33
    Materials 33
    Preparing and Measuring the Tank 34
    Making The Tank 35
    Folding The Plastic 36
    Forming the Ice Surface 38
Maintaining the Ice Surface 38
Lighting 39
Suggestions for Managing Your Rink 39

CHAPTER 4 / BASIC SKATING SKILLS 43

Stepping Out for the First Time 44
Falling Down.. 46
Getting Up 47
Competition and Learning 49
On-ice Supports 49

CHAPTER 5 / SKATING FORWARD **51**
Gliding and Gentle Turns 52
Pulling and Gliding 52
Pushing and Gliding 53
Gliding and Turning 53
From the Basics To... 54
Gliding, Sitting and Standing 55
Gliding with Skates Different Widths Apart 55
Other Activities 56
    Sculling Forward 56
    The T-Push and Glide 57
    Stroking 59
    Playing Aeroplane 60
    Chasing the Ball 60
    Skating Around The Marker 61
Warming Up and Cooling Down 62

CHAPTER 6 / STOPPING **63**
The Snowplow 64
Freeze Tag.. 65
Obstacle Course 66
Catch-up 66
The Hockey Stop 67
Skate/Stop/Skate 69
Reversing the Directions 69

CHAPTER 7 / FORWARD STRIDING **71**
The V-Start... 72
Pushing and Gliding 73
Games... 74

CHAPTER 8 / SKATING BACKWARDS **77**
Beginning Steps 79
Coasting Backwards 79
Coasting Backwards for Distance 79

Sculling Backwards 80
Starting Backwards: The C-cut 82
Stroking Backwards 83
Stopping while Skating Backwards 84
    Backwards Tag 85
    Big Circle 85
    Zig-zag 86

CHAPTER 9 / TURNING AND EDGE CONTROL **87**
Over to You 88
Skate Edges 88
Scooting 90
Cross-Overs 91
Circles 93
Figure-8 93
Train 94
Weaving or Slalom 94
Circle Tag 94
Sharper Turns 95
Guess the Direction 95

CHAPTER 10 / INTERMEDIATE SKATING SKILLS **97**
Pivoting 98
Standing Forward Pivot 99
Forward Pivot—Moving 100
Backward Pivot—Moving 102
Moving Sideways 103
Timing Your Drills 108
Tight Turns 109
Tandem 111
Turning Around A Friend 111
Timed Turns 111
Relays 111
The Backward T-Stop 112

CHAPTER 11 / BASIC PUCKHANDLING SKILLS **113**
The Basic Puckhandling Position 114
Stationary Puckhandling 115
An Important Note about Puck Control 116
Skating Forward with the Puck 117
Random Skating 118

Weaving with the Puck 118
Retrieving a Stationary Puck 118
Starting with the Puck 119
Skating Backwards with the Puck 119
    Keepaway 119
    Zig-zag 119
    Pig in the Middle 120
Stopping with the Puck 120

CHAPTER 12 / PASSING AND RECEIVING **123**
Stationary Forehand Passing and Shooting 124
Stationary Backhand Passing 125
Receiving a Pass 126
Leading the Skater 128
Skating and Passing 129
Forward and Backward 130
Weave and Shoot 131

CHAPTER 13 / IN-LINE SKATING BASICS **133**
In-Line Skating and Hockey 136
Differences between In-Line Skating and Ice Skating 136
Equipment and Safety 137
Homemade Alternatives to In-Line Skating Equipment ... 138
Selecting the Right Type of Skate 139
Fitting Your Skates 140
Safety Tips 142
Surfaces 143
Maintenance of In-Line Skates 144

CHAPTER 14 / IN-LINE SKATING SKILLS **145**
First Steps: Stepping out and Stopping 146
Your First Steps 146
Learning to Stop 148
Stopping Using the Heel Brake 149
Advanced In-Line Skating Skills 152
Direction Changes 153
Pivoting 153
Backward Skating 153
Roller-Hockey 154

FURTHER READING **155**

SYMBOLS

The following symbols are used in diagrams throughout the book.

Pylon or marker	Hockey stick
Starting position	Ordinary wooden sticks
Finishing position	Step or jump over
Stop	Wood on top of pylon (to step or jump over)
Skating with the puck	Player
Skating forwards	Lateral movement
Skating backwards	Puck
	Shooting/passing the puck

1
The Backyard Rink Approach

BILL KEAY

The Backyard Rink Approach — Introduction

"It is preferable to have the beginner learn hockey in a program that provides the proper balance between skill progression and fun, than to have him learn only through regularly scheduled hockey playing in a highly organized series of games with little or no emphasis on skill development."
—George Lariviere, *Beginner's Program—Hockey Development Council*

Ice hockey is arguably the national game of Canada. It is also considered to be the fastest game in the world. We have become accustomed to the "razzle-dazzle" of professional hockey games on television, but many of us have forgotten the humble origins of this great game.

The game of ice hockey that we know today originally evolved from the Europeans who settled in Canada in the 1800s. They played "shinny" on frozen ponds, lakes or rivers, often shooting into netless goals made from two pieces of wood stuck into the ice

Today countless Canadians continue this rural tradition by playing make-up games on ponds, community rinks, or even on ice surfaces made in our backyards. A number of the top players in the National Hockey League began their careers on home-made rinks in backyards or empty neighbourhood lots.

There are community leagues and levels of organized hockey now available for children, largely as a result of the efforts of Amateur Hockey Associations across North America. However, many parents and children have returned to the less formal backyard rink approach to learning hockey and skating skills for a number of reasons:

• the backyard rink approach focuses on learning, fun and family involvement, which are the essence of childhood;

• the backyard rink approach is cheaper than most organized hockey programs, since there are no fees for ice-time and registration, and equipment costs are less (e.g., no uniforms);

• parents and children have more time to participate in a variety of other recreational activities that are of interest to them;

• a backyard rink approach minimizes the time involved in transporting kids to and from organized practices and games;

• parents and kids are not tied down to any formal competition schedule;

• ice is easily available in the home-rink approach;

• if practices at home are well organized, kids get the maximum ice time to actively practice their skills, as opposed to sitting on a bench watching others do them, as can often happen in organized hockey;

• there are no team selection cuts, which means more kids can learn these skills;

• the backyard rink approach allows young players to develop hockey skills without the negative influence of distorted perspectives about "winning", which can occasionally creep into organized hockey. Too much of a focus on winning can sometimes lead to aggressive and dangerous behaviour by parents and children, both on and off the ice. A focus on winning at the expense of fun and enjoyment can decrease a child's desire to remain involved in the game.

• the backyard rink approach to learning can help to increase a child's self-confidence, by helping them to compare their improvements against their own past performances. Children will gain confidence from the results of their own efforts, rather than comparing themselves against others, which can often happen in the competitive situation.

"When I was a youngster, we played on an open-air rink; to get it started we needed a snow-storm, six or even ten inches …We'd all go out, the kids, their fathers, the fans, and pat it down with shovels and stomp the snow until it was a flat surface…we'd get a hose and flood it again and again. I can remember my father going out at midnight to flood an open-air rink for Tony and me. In the morning, unless it snowed during the night, it would be great. I used to love flooding the rink, but I wasn't too happy when we had to plow it off."
—Phil Esposito (1976) *Phil Esposito's Winning Hockey for Beginners*. Henry Regnery Company: Chicago

About This Book

The best time for children to learn the basics of ice hockey is between the ages of four and eleven years. This book is aimed at the parents of those young children who are just taking their first steps in skates. We have described one alternative to organized hockey by providing a program of hockey skills for *everyone* that can be practiced at home.

Chapter Two gives some ideas on how to reduce the cost of equipment.

In Chapter Three we've included some ways of building a skating rink in your own backyard. This minimizes travel time, and allows your children plenty of opportunities to practice. Ice is also available all day every day in the winter, at very little cost.

Once your child is equipped and the rink is flooded, cleared off and ready to go, it's time to step out onto the ice.

In Chapters Four through Twelve we outline some ideas for the development of a natural progression of skating and puckhandling skills, so that you as a parent and coach can guide your child through the basics.

You will find suggestions for teaching and practicing the skills needed for forward and backward skating, stopping and turning, and passing and shooting the puck.

Finally, we have included two chapters for the beginning in-line skater. In Chapters Thirteen and Fourteen, we offer tips on safety and equipment, and discuss some differences between ice-skating and in-line skating. We also suggest some ice-skating skill progressions which can be used to learn and practice in-line skating.

We hope that the ideas in this book will open up opportunities to children who have not yet had the chance to skate and play hockey. By the time your child reaches the level of competence shown at the end of the book, they will be ready to join a competitive hockey league, if they wish.

How Children Develop Skills

Children develop physical skills in a slow, gradual and orderly pattern. A child naturally progresses through the increasingly difficult and predictable phases of creeping, crawling and standing, before walking.

Hockey and skating skills are learned in a similar manner.

A child who is beginning to skate will need support from an adult during those first few times on the ice. With practice and encouragement, the child passes through to the natural phases of shuffling along the ice without support, and gliding while being pulled or pushed along, until finally they are able to propel themselves along under their own power.

As the child develops skill and strength, and gains confidence from past successes, they will eventually get closer and closer to skillful skating. There is a fairly natural progressive order of skills through which a child passes in order to acquire skating skill. This progression takes time, since a child has to develop the strength, balance and coordination needed for a high level of performance.

If you are a good skater, can you remember how long it took *you* to learn to skate well?

Although every child goes through a similar order or sequence of skills, there often is a difference between the levels of skill shown by children of the same age, or of different ages. Those differences are due to many reasons, but primarily to:

"But it didn't come easy for Wayne Gretzky. He practiced very hard...for years. Every fall Walter Gretzky would set up a sprinkler in the Gretzky backyard in Brantford, Ontario. All night long the sprinkler would run. Night after night in the freezing Canadian winters. The entire backyard would become as smooth as glass with ice. It would become a do-it-yourself ice-skating rink. That's where a determined Wayne Gretzky practiced and practiced."
—Russ Olney (1982). *Winners! Super Champions of Ice Hockey.* New York: Clarion Books.

15

- the amount of skating practice they've had;
- how well they take to the activity;
- whether or not they receive patient encouragement while they learn.

We know that children differ in their inherited physical capacities. More importantly, we know that the child's learning environment, the opportunity to practice, and their feelings about the activity are also very important factors in aiding the development of any sport skill.

The Learning Environment

Any learning is helped if parents, teachers, coaches and the child's peers provide a positive, supportive and encouraging learning environment. In such an atmosphere children can try and experiment with new skills, without the fear that they will be ridiculed or punished if they don't succeed.

Feedback on the child's performance of a skill should be given in a non-critical manner. Good habits and skilled performance should be encouraged with praise and attention. Bad habits can be brought to the child's attention in a matter-of-fact manner, and without punishment. The child should be encouraged for having tried, told simply what was done wrong, and then given tips on how to improve the skill.

Remember, with plenty of practice and a little guidance, your child will naturally develop the required skills. Too often we forget that children are not miniature adults. Children are smaller, less skillful and less strong than their adult counterparts. Equipment and playing surfaces should be scaled down to children's size.

Children are also less mature psychologically. They

have a shorter attention span than adults, and are not as able to plan and forsee the consequences of their actions. Formal practice times or instructional periods should be kept short, and the child allowed to learn by enjoyable practice and play. Games and activities should also be described clearly.

The Importance of Practice and Skill Level

Children should be given plenty of opportunity to practice hockey skills at a time when they are *ready* and *willing* to learn them. New skills should be presented at the child's individual developmental level.

If we ask a child to do a task that is too far beyond their current level of ability it will probably lead to frustration and discouragement. You may have experienced this if a friend led you down a difficult ski run on your first day on skis! Such negative, failure experiences decrease an adult's or child's self-confidence.

Likewise, if we ask children to do something that's too easy they can easily become bored. You should observe the child at play to determine their level of ability, and teach them to try new skills at or just above that level.

In Chapters Four through Twelve you will find a number of skating and puckhandling skills, presented in *increasing* order of difficulty. You can use this as a guide to gauging your child's present developmental level.

Remember, practice ensures development of skill.

Fun and Play Keep Boredom Away!

If a child enjoys the skills they are learning, and has fun learning them, they will be encouraged to do more and more. Motivation, or your child's willingness to practice, is also helped by comparing their present performance to their own previous performances, and not to the performances of other children who may be more or less advanced at any given time.

When we can see the improvement in our abilities resulting from our own hard efforts we are usually encouraged to practice more. Comparison to other people, who are much more able than we, often leads to discouragement, or resentment.

Much of our best learning occurs through self-directed play and exploration. In this book, we have included many games and activities that you and your child can do to have fun and practice the skills. You will also find suggestions for timing your child's performance during some of those activities, and evaluating those times to show improvements with practice.

Too often as adults and parents we can take the fun out of learning for children. Developing basic skating and puckhandling skills in a fun, positive environment will go a long way towards helping your child learn, and to maintaining a continued interest in Canada's national game.

2
Equipment

Children's Hockey Equipment

Before children first step onto the ice, it is important that they have the proper equipment.

For many of us the cost of equipment can be prohibitive, but with a little ingenuity we can minimize the cost and give our children the opportunity to play. Many of the more expensive, manufactured items can be homemade (see page 25).

However, you will still have to buy (or borrow) a pair of skates and a hockey stick.

Ice Skates

A child's feet grow quickly, so your young skater may need a new pair of skates each year. Therefore, you may want to buy second-hand skates, or swap skates with a friend or neighbour. You might also pick up second-hand skates at a garage sale.

Young children cause very little wear in one season so a used pair that fits well will often be just as good as an expensive pair. If you want to provide a community program you may want to set up a 'loaner' program and charge a minimal fee for the rental of skates.

However you decide to get your skates, be sure that they fit your child well:

• the skating boot may be the same size, or up to half a size smaller than your walking shoes;

• the skates should not be too tight, and should be fitted when your child is wearing thick socks. If the boot is too tight the blood supply to the foot is cut off, causing pain and discomfort;

• the boot should hold the heel, instep and ankle snugly

and comfortably;
- when fitted properly there should be room for the toes to wiggle.

Caring for Your Skates

To keep your skates in good condition, follow these guidelines:
- always dry the skate blades after skating;
- waterproof or polish the boots to keep them watertight;
- wear guards on the blades when you're not on the ice;
- keep skates sharp for better control in all skating movements.

Clothing

Almost any regular street clothing can be worn when practicing hockey and skating skills. Here are some things to think about:
- the child should be warm and comfortable. Winter clothes that keep the child good and warm also provide padding to cushion the inevitable falls;
- clothing should be in *layers*, so that one or two layers can be taken off if the child gets too warm;
- the clothing should *not* be so tight or bulky that it gets in the way, and restricts the child's movement.

Helmet

A good helmet is a necessity nowadays for bicycling, ice skating and in-line skating (See Chapter Thirteen: In-Line Skating Basics).

You can use one helmet for all these activities and save money. A bicycle helmet would suffice for *all* these

"Bobby [Orr] got his first pair of skates when he was four years old. They were given to him as a present by a friend of his father. The skates were secondhand and not very fancy, but to Bobby they might have well been made of solid gold. He grinned with pleasure when he saw them. He learned to use them on the frozen Sequin River. At first his ankles were too weak to support him. When he tried to stand up on the blades of his skates, his ankles wobbled and collapsed beneath his weight.
—Sue & Marshall Burchard (1973). *Sports Hero— Bobby Orr*. New York: G.P. Putnam & Sons.

activities. We also suggest that an ice-hockey helmet with its cage removed would be suitable for in-line skating.

When buying a helmet here are some things to watch for:

• when you are fitting the helmet make sure it fits snugly—the better the fit of the helmet, the better the protection;

• the helmet should cover the top of the forehead and fit squarely on top of the head;

• helmets that fall off the back of the head, or drop down over the eyebrows, are not fitted properly. The snug fit should ensure that the helmet does not move from side to side, or slide down over your child's eyes—a helmet that is too big could easily fall off during an accident, or could impair their field of vision if it slips forward;

• the chin strap should be done up to fit snugly—not too loose or too tight;

• small sticky-backed sizing pads can be found at most stores that sell helmets—these pads can be arranged to provide a snug fit to helmets that are a little too large, thus allowing the purchase of a helmet with some room for your child's head to grow.

The Stick

When buying a stick for yourself or your child there are some things to look for:

• make sure the stick is the right length;

• when wearing skates, hold the shaft of the stick vertically with the tip (toe) of the stick blade on the ice;

• the butt-end of the shaft should come to about the chin.

Some players will prefer a slightly longer stick, others a slightly shorter one—the player should be allowed to make the choice. In most cases you'll have to cut a few inches off of the shaft (handle) to make it the right length.

When a young player stands (wearing skates) gripping the stick in both hands, with a slight bend at the knees and

Finding the correct stick length.

waist, the blade should be flat on the ice. Let your child try several sticks to find the lie that feels most comfortable when the blade is flat on the ice.

For the first few seasons, the stick should have a straight blade without a curve. This will make it much easier to learn to control the puck, and it will allow the young player to try *both* a left handed and a right handed grip.

The hand that is lower on the shaft indicates the *shooting* side. When the right hand is lower, the player shoots

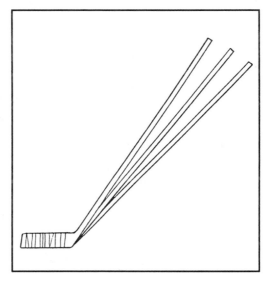

The lie of the blade: the angle that the blade makes with the shaft—or handle—of the stick.

"The Dryden saga began on the streets of Islington, Ontario...where young, angular Ken played ball hockey using goals made of two-by-fours and chicken wire."
—Stan Fischler (1978). *Kings of the Rink.* New York: Dodd, Mead & Company.

right-handed. Their left hand will be at the top of the shaft guiding the stick.

Left-handers will have the left hand lower and the right hand at the top.

The right-handed shooter places the blade on the ice on the right side of the body. When they shoot or pass the puck from this position they are using their *forehand*—the puck is in contact with the front of the blade.

When they keep the same grip but switch the blade over to the left side, and shoot or pass forward, they are using their *backhand*—the puck is in contact with the back of the blade.

While most players quickly identify which grip feels better, some lucky young people will discover they can handle the stick well on *either* side. To be ambidextrous in this way is a real advantage when playing hockey.

Left-handed and right-handed players, seen from behind.

Homemade Alternatives to Regular Hockey Equipment

Many regularly manufactured items can be made at home. A bicycle helmet could double as a hockey helmet, and regular leather gloves become an alternative to expensive hockey gloves. Woollen mitts over leather or cloth gloves, or even two pairs of woollen mitts, will provide padding and protection, as well as insulating against the cold.

Skates .... no alternative, but could be borrowed, bought second-hand or traded.

Sticks .... no alternative—use a child's stick.

Knee Pads ..... an old pair of socks cut off and padded.

Rear Pad .... a towel stuffed in the seat of the pants.

Pants .... regular old pants, and long underwear.

Stockings .... a long pair of thick socks.

Helmet .... a bicycle helmet.

Gloves .... leather mitts, ringette gloves, work mitts or regular gloves.

Cup .... not needed.

Pucks .... street puck, ice puck, a ball hockey ball or tennis ball.

Pylons .... an empty *plastic* soap, detergent or cooking oil container, with two inches of water frozen in the bottom. *Never use metal cans or glass bottles* for pylons or anything else on the ice. This can result in serious cuts, and glass is even more brittle than usual in the cold, and breaks easily.

Goal .... a homemade or street-hockey goal. Make it out of metal piping or wood, and netting. Use a target of pylons, or piles of snow. You can also tape or paint marks on the boards, or even use canvas and wood.

3

Making a Homemade Rink

JOEL RUSS

"Every winter, his dad would mow the backyard to a stubble and spend nine days forming an ice rink. At the age of two, Wayne [Gretzky] was skating on what he later called, 'the best ice in Canada'."
—Nathan Aaseng (1984) *Hockey's Super Scorers.* Minneapolis: Lerner Publications.

Location

A homemade rink can be made anywhere that the ground is flat and even. Possible locations include:
- a local unused lot;
- an outdoor tennis or basketball court;
- or, most conveniently, your own backyard.

The surface can be grass or concrete. Turf is the most common surface under an outdoor rink, although artificial surfaces are best since the surface is usually smooth and even. If you are using a concrete or hard artificial surface, be sure that there aren't any large cracks that might be opened up even more by the action of frozen water.

Effects of Ice on Grass

People are often cautious about putting a rink on their grass, since they are worried about how much damage might be caused by the ice. The debate continues about the effects of ice on grass, and it seems to be a matter of luck as to the amount of damage caused. Quite a few people who have built homemade rinks report that their grass remains unaffected, even after several winter's use.

If you are worried about damage to turf, here are some tips to follow:
- construct your rink on a garden patch or earth base;
- place it on a piece of grass that you aren't worried about.

To prevent damage, turf should be as hardy as possible, so finish watering and fertilizing in the middle of August. Succulent, growing grass is more likely to become more damaged than hardy grass that has stopped growing for the season. Also:

- make sure that the rink is near a water outlet with an inside shut-off valve to prevent freezing.

Ideally, you should place the rink out of the prevailing winds. If possible, also try to place the rink in the shade from the sun.

Preparing the Site

Once you have decided on your location, make sure the site is kept as clear and as even as possible. An uneven surface can increase water usage very significantly–think of a bath tub with a low end or corner!

Remove large rocks and stones up to 6-8 inches in depth from earth areas. Stones trap and retain heat causing "local" melting spots in the ice. They can also prevent the formation of an even ice surface.

Grass should be cut as short as possible before flooding. Any loose grass should also be raked off. Before the temperature reaches freezing, flood or spray the ground once a week to enable the frost to set in.

Sprinkling the grass with snow to a depth of 1-2 inches may also protect the grass.

The Size of the Rink

Some people suggest a minimum rink size of 50x100 feet. However, a home rink of 40x35 feet is excellent for learning to skate and for children's games, and is within the means of many homeowners. While rectangular rinks are the most usual, any shape will do. Some people even use areas where large trees are incorporated into the ice surface!

"[Billy Smith's father] coached his boys during their younger days and spared no effort to see that they got a chance to practice hockey. He painted houses to get money for equipment, shoveled snow off the backyard rink before going to work, and strung lights over the rink so his sons could practice at night."
—Nathan Aaseng (1984) *Hockey's Fearless Goalies.* Minneapolis: Lerner Publications.

Types of Rink

Traditionally, there are two methods of building a rink.

The first method, called the *bordered-off method*, involves spraying or flooding a bordered-off area of grass, turf or asphalt.

The second method, called the *tank method*, uses a tank made out of wood and plastic sheeting.

The following sections explain in detail how to make a rink using *both* of these methods. You will also find complete materials lists for each method, and a series of diagrams to assist you.

The Bordered-Off Rink

Materials

- 1x8-inch planking.
- 12-inch stakes.
- 1/4 pound of galvanized 1 1/2 inch nails.

Creating the Border

The preparation of the borders should be done *before* the ground freezes, to make inserting the stakes easier.

The basic shape of the rink can be outlined by taut strings. The designated rink area can be surrounded by wooden boards or snow banks to prevent the leakage of water from the rink.

Planks can be laid out end-to-end around the strings. The planks can be held in place by the stakes, which are set 4 inches into the ground.

The stakes can then be placed in the ground along the

string line, at the intersection of two planks. The planks can now be nailed to the stakes.

Remember to nail the planks from the inside of the rink. This prevents any scratches or cuts from the nails.

Once all the boards are up and some snow has fallen, you can seal the inside *and* the outside of the boards with snow.

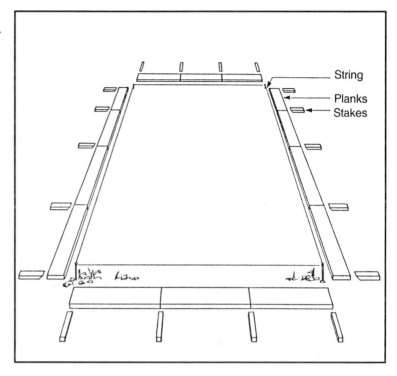

String
Planks
Stakes

How to prepare the outline of a simple rink.

Forming the Ice Surface

On those first cold nights (colder than -5°C or 25°F), try not to overspray the skating area. Sprinkle the area lightly with a hose equipped with a spray nozzle, or even a lawn sprinkler. The lawn sprinkler must be of the *random broadcaster* type, since water will freeze in the spray pattern of an ordinary sprinkler. This early, light spraying creates a hard base for future ice.

If possible, use a 1 or 1 1/4 inch hose designed for cold weather use. An ordinary 3/4-inch *rubber* hose works best since plastic hoses become brittle in cold temperatures.

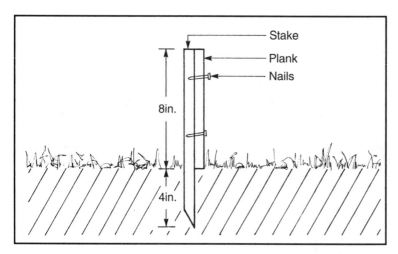

Stake
Plank
Nails
8in.
4in.

Positions of the stakes, planks and nails.

Sealing the boards with snow.

Once you have hardened the ground, spray the area until the ice is 3 1/2 to 4 inches deep to form a *sealing coat.*

Additional ice should be added half an inch at a time. For larger rinks, spray in strips 12 -15 feet wide, backwards from the farthest point in the rink.

Continue to spray until the surface is covered. Let fresh water flow to the mark of the last ice to aid in forming an even coat. Remember, water finds its own level.

Sprinklers may become blocked with ice if the weather is very cold.

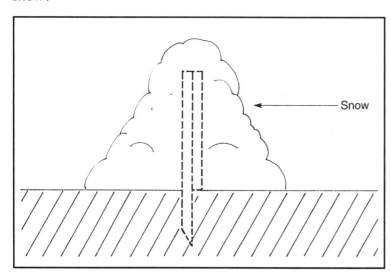

Snow

Flooding

To maintain a smooth skating surface, your rink will need to be flooded regularly.

Once the sealing coat has been formed, the skating area can be flooded up to a depth of three or depth of three or four inches and allowed to freeze.

The 50 x 100 foot rink could become a "life's work" to flood using a hose, so perhaps the flooding method would be more suitable for a smaller rink.

Either drain the hose before putting it away, or store it in a warm basement. The latter is preferable since you will be very cold after a flooding session, and you'll probably want to get indoors to get warm. Draining a hose outside on the ground can be hazardous, as it can result in the creation of casual ice, and draining it on the rink can often get you wet!

A different method of rink construction which exclusively uses this technique is known as the *tank method*.

The Tank Method

Thanks to Dr. Art Burgess, Faculty of Physical Education & Recreation Studies, University of Alberta, for telling us about this method which he has used with great success for many years.

The tank method involves creating a shallow wading pool that will hold water to a depth of six inches. This method helps protect the grass from freezing since the ice is contained in a plastic tank.

Materials

The tank method of constructing a rink requires:
 • 1x8 inch boards, construction grade—lineal footage to equal the perimeter of the rink, plus 10% extra
 • 18-inch (1"x2") garden stakes—stakes are placed at five-foot intervals. You can butt two boards end-to-end

with one stake, but it is easier to place stakes side-by-side and nail the boards to them, so for a 20x40-foot rink, you'll need about 50 stakes.

- 1/4 pound of galvanized 1 1/2 inch nails.
- 0.04m polythene plastic sheeting. This is produced in 20x100-foot rolls. Usually the supplier will sell 20-foot widths by the lineal foot.
- 1/2-inch construction staples (not office staples).
- 3/4x3/4 inch wooden washers. These can be cut from the 1x8 inch scraps. The washers are used to prevent the staples from being pulled through the plastic.
- acoustic cement—1 tube for each 40 feet of seam.

Preparing and Measuring the Tank

The area should first be surveyed and cleared.

The rink can be laid out with right-angled corners, using strings. If the ground is uneven, the area can be made level by spreading wood shavings in the low spots.

The size of the plastic sheeting will define the width of the rink. Since the sheeting usually comes in 20 foot widths, two sheets will result in a rink width of about 37 feet. Remember—three of those feet are taken up by folding the two sheets together to make a water-tight seam.

If you have space, you could use three plastic sheets with two water-tight seams. This would give you a rink width of about 55 1/2 feet.

The length of the rink depends on the space that is available, and it could be as long as the 100 foot roll of plastic. Therefore, measure the available area and buy the appropriate amount of sheeting.

Note: Construction should be done before the weather turns too cold since:

- it is more comfortable to work, and
- it's very difficult to put stakes into frozen ground.

Making the Tank

Put the stakes in the ground at the appropriate intervals, and attach the boards securely to them. This can be done by laying the boards alongside the strings (see The Bordered-Off Rink).

This provides a framework on which to mount the tank. You may want to lay the plastic out first so you know how much space you will need.

Roll out the plastic sheeting along the length of the rink, leaving enough at each end to staple to the boards.

Don't staple at this point! The plastic should be cut at right angles to the boards. There should be enough plastic to cover the grass, and to line the inside of the boards.

How to attach the plastic sheeting to the boards.

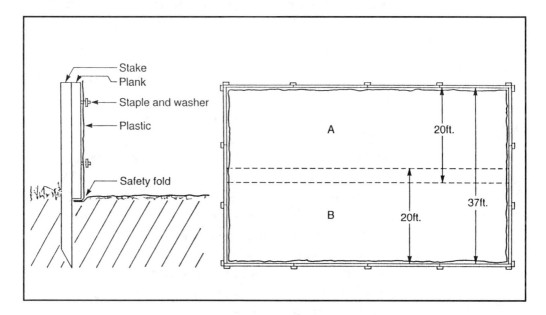

35

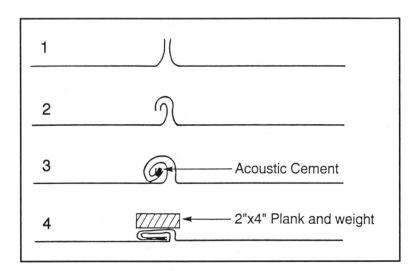

Folding the plastic.

Folding the Plastic

Notice that there is a safety fold tucked just underneath the boards. This helps to prevent the weight of the water from pulling the plastic out from the staples.

Once the sheeting is laid out, make sure you have enough to line the boards. Create a safety fold, and make an overlap of one and a half feet in the middle between the two lengths of plastic.

The folding of the plastic will take two people, and goes as follows:

• lap the fold material of A sheet with B sheet (1) (see illustration on page 35);

• the first fold will take half of the overlap, and should be done carefully so as to keep the seam straight (2);

• the second fold should be cemented with a continuous bead of acoustic cement—allow no breaks (3);

• fold the seam over again, and cement it as before (4);

• place weights along the length of the seam to help the acoustic cement to set (4);

• leave for 24 hours.

After 24 hours, turn the entire joined sheet over so that the folded lap and seams are on the underside. Now, the water

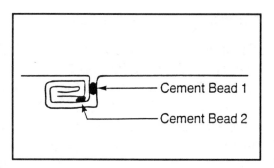

Cement Bead 1

Cement Bead 2

How to fold the plastic sheeting.

pressure will force the folds and seams shut, thus giving a complete seal.

Staple the plastic to the boards with construction staples placed through 3/4 inch x 3/4 inch wooden washers (see illustration on page 35). The washers can be cut from 1 inch x 8 inch scraps. You need not use the washers, but they do prevent the plastic from tearing.

The corners of the sheeting can be folded like those of a bed sheet, and then stapled. It is wise to fix all staples at the upper edge of the boards, in order to avoid any leakage from lower down.

If one end of the tank is low (e.g., if the rink is on a sloping surface), it may be necesary to build a double height of boards, and carry the plastic up higher.

A good tip: when making the tank, it is wise to work in soft shoes or even stocking feet, if the weather permits. The more the plastic is walked on, the greater the chance there is for puncture to occur.

Forming the Ice Surface

The tank can be filled with water using a garden hose, as one would fill a wading pool.

Once filled, it can be left for the first freezing weather to create the ice. The tank could be built over a late October weekend, and then left as an attractive reflecting pool and bird-bath until freezing temperatures turn it into a skating rink.

It is not necessary or desirable to fill the tank to the top. Put in enough water to give one and a half inches of ice at the shallowest points. This allows room for later flooding without overflowing the boards.

Try to keep leaves and other dark objects out of the water. In a warm sun these become "hot spots" which melt the ice, making it uneven and dangerous.

Maintaining the Ice Surface

Now that you have your ice surface, whether it be a bordered-off or tank-style rink, here are some tips to help keep it in good condition:

• always sweep any excess snow from the ice before skating or adding more water to the surface;

• keep the ice clear of stones, broken ice or leaves;

• use a wide-blade snow scraper or even a homemade plywood type to keep the surface clear, but store it well away from the ice surface so there is no chance someone might fall or be pushed over it and get injured;

• check the boards or edging to be sure that nails or other dangerous objects won't cause injury or tear clothing in case of a spill;

• if the rink is bordered partly by a yard fence check it too, so that any nails or splinters are removed;

- the area by the boards or snow borders should also be kept clear, so that ice doesn't build up or form a rough surface there;
- keep any snowbanks around the area as low as possible, since high banks help to form hard-packed snowdrifts which are difficult to clear;
- you may find that the ice surface may need to be watered three times a week to create an optimum surface.

Lighting

Lighting for nighttime skating can be provided by a wide angle, all-weather floodlight. Alternatively, the rink might be surrounded by white Christmas-tree lights.

Suggestions for Managing Your Rink

An outdoor rink in your backyard is a lot of fun for all concerned, and if one is careful it can be a lot less of a problem than might be expected.

The first step is to lay out some simple rules and see that they are enforced. You may want to change some of these and add some of your own, but these are a start.

The rink is for fun and learning.

Children who fight or argue continually must leave the rink for that day. They can come back the next day if they agree to behave. If the situation gets too rough-and-tumble or out of hand, the only measure necessary to ensure safe, enjoyable play is to have the troublemaker sit out of the action for a while.

Everyone who uses the rink, no matter how young, should help to keep it cleared of snow, scraped off and

flooded, so that the surface is in good condition.

There is always something that can be done to help, even by the youngest child.

Consider using different age limits for different times of the day or week.

Depending on the numbers and ages of your family and neighbourhood kids, you might want to restrict access to skaters under 6 years of age for certain periods, or 6 to 10 years, or over 10 years, for particular times.

It is also useful at times to restrict use to skaters without sticks, so that the emphasis can be on skating balance and control. Any such restrictions can be announced on a homemade sign mounted near the rink on a fence or simple post.

Plywood covers for windows that may be in the line of fire can avoid costly window replacements.

Very light pucks are safe in this respect and provide plenty of challenge to control. Tennis or other small balls can help to develop control skills and are less dangerous than full-size pucks. If you can find pucks of standard rubber that are smaller than regulation pucks, you should get several—they are safer and easier to handle for young skaters.

Girls and boys of many ages can play safely together, provided the emphasis is on fun.

If necessary, set a limit to the number of children that may be on the ice at one time. Once the limit is reached, additional children arriving to play will have to wait in turn until someone leaves or comes off to rest for a while.

You may especially want to limit the number of skaters

on the ice when hockey sticks are used. If a rink gets too crowded, sticks can be dangerous.

Children other than your own should observe common courtesy by asking for permission to use the rink.

You could make an easel-type sign that says something like "Rink Open—You're Welcome" and another that says "Rink Closed—Please Stay Off."

Neighbourhood children should understand that it is a privilege to use the rink. Of course, if your yard has a sturdy, high fence with a secure gate that locks, this will simplify matters.

If you build a rink one year that is open to children of other families, you may want to see if someone else will take on the job the next year.

A vacant lot or the corner of an open area may be located close to several families who could share in the building and maintaining of a simple rink.

You might consider talking with an insurance agent or lawyer concerning questions of liability in regard to your backyard rink.

4

Basic Skating Skills

Some of the ideas we present in the next chapters have been adapted from a variety of sources. These sources, and ideas for further study, are listed in the *Further Reading* section at the end of the book.

Stepping Out for the First Time

Now that your young skater is equipped, it's time to get out onto the ice.

If this is one of their first times on the ice your child will need some help in standing and lots of encouragement, praise and patience. Remember, this should be a *fun* experience for both you and your child, but it can also be very frightening, as you may recall.

Your child will want plenty of time to just get the feeling of standing on the ice with their weight on both skates. Share in their excitement and help give them a sense of security by providing secure support, and plenty of praise and encouragement.

Try any one of the following methods of support:
- stand beside the child, holding the closer hand;
- reach behind to take the other hand at shoulder height. This lets them see in front of them;
- stand behind or in front of them, holding both of their hands at *their* shoulder height;
- stand behind or in front of the skater, while both of you hold onto the shaft of a hockey or broom stick or a thin piece of wood;
- stand beside them and hold *one* hand, if their balance is good enough.

*The illustrations
on this page
demonstrate four
different ways to
support your
child.*

Focus on enjoyment and try to resist giving instructions.
There will be plenty of time for that later!

What your child needs at this stage is simply to experience this new and unpredictable situation, along with a few friendly suggestions.

Remember the first few weeks when your child started to walk? They didn't need instruction—what they needed was protection against painful falls, and for you to share in their excitement in those new accomplishments.

In early walking your child not only wanted, but *needed*, to hold one or both of your hands. Gradually, over a few weeks, they needed less and less help, and then only in particularly difficult spots. Once your child gained confidence they insisted on striking out on their own. That will soon happen here too.

So don't rush these first few steps. Let your child set the pace, and wait until they get used to things.

Remember, they might either be very excited or very frightened—or a little of both. When *they're* ready to start moving, let them—whether that's as soon as you step onto the ice, or after settling down a bit.

The first movement is almost always cautious—walking with the skates kept close to the ice, shuffling, or partly sliding down the ice.

As your skater shows a greater willingness to work on their own, let them. Just stay close enough to avoid dangerous spills.

Falling Down

During this initial phase it's useful to tell a child how to fall. First, tell them it's okay to fall; everyone does it. Explain that when they feel their feet going out from under them, just try to relax and allow themselves to sink forward to the ice by bending the knees.

Falling down happens to everyone.

Getting Up

If other skaters are on the ice, it is important that the child gets up as soon as possible so nobody trips over them.

To get up, they can:

• roll over onto one hip with both hands and one knee on the ice;

• bring the other leg in underneath them;

• place the blade of one skate firmly on the ice, then raise themselves up into a standing position.

If they try to get up from a sitting or lying position by putting their weight on both skates, their feet will come out from underneath them.

It is important, as with all skating skills, that your child can get up from both left and right sides. They can even practice getting up from a face down position on the ice, but make sure they don't get too cold or wet.

Rolling over to get up.

Getting up from the kneeling position.

Children will have mastered this skill when they can get up on their own, but they will need some assistance at first.

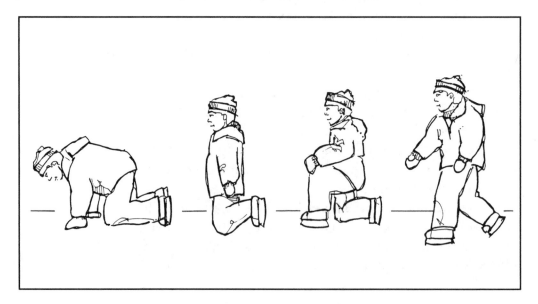

Competition and Learning

If there are other children learning with your child, do not make comparisons or create competition at this stage. The child who progresses rapidly this early will not necessarily become the best skater in the long run. Competition during the early stages of learning takes the child's attention away from their own efforts, and focuses it on what others are doing, or makes them worry about keeping up.

If the child wants to compete, there will be plenty of opportunity later. At this stage, children love to share the excitement with others who are learning too. If two or more children *all want* to compete in some simple things, by all means let them. What is harmful is forcing children who are not ready, or simply don't want to compete.

On-ice Supports

When your child shows signs of wanting some more freedom, let them try using the boards for support (if there are any), or a cardboard or wooden box of at least waist height, or a chair or "walker-type" support. Initially, the parent can help the skater by gently pulling the object.

It is important to get your child practicing these basic skating skills *without* a hockey stick.

Walking using a support.

49

Giving a child a stick to handle will focus attention away from the skating skill, and probably make a task that is difficult enough even more demanding. More important, a beginner will use the stick for support rather than developing their own sense of balance. Creating a sense of balance on the ice is *crucial* at this stage.

The skilled skater has excellent body balance, and when playing hockey the stick is used to control the puck, *not* for balance.

5
Skating Forward

Gliding and Gentle Turns

Once your child has become confident enough to be pulled along with sticks or to walk around the rink on their own, they are ready to learn to glide.

The best stance for skating and gliding is shown below. It is very important to practice gliding without a stick, so that the learner does not become dependent on it for balance.

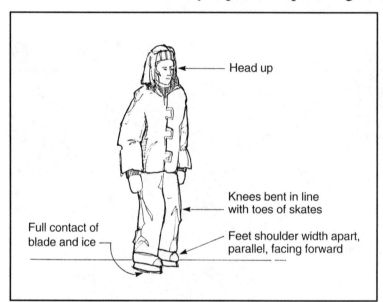

Head up

Knees bent in line with toes of skates

Feet shoulder width apart, parallel, facing forward

Full contact of blade and ice

The basic skating stance.

The best skaters control their movement and balance without relying on the stick, which can then be used to control the puck or to check with.

Here are some fun things for your child to try:

- balancing on two feet, then on one foot;
- some little jumps up and down.

Pulling and Gliding

Gently pull your child along the ice. Let them try the basic stance. Don't worry if they don't get it the first time, just let them experiment.

Next, pull them along with two hockey sticks. This will give them a little more independence.

52

Pulling and gliding (left); pushing and gliding (below).

Pushing and Gliding

Gently push your young skater from behind. Let go, and allow them to glide on their own. See for how many counts, or for how far, they can keep going.

Encourage them to increase the duration of the glide, and try to help them keep their skate blades flat on the ice.

Gliding and Turning

Ask your child to glide and turn gently in either direction. Mark out a course with pylons or plastic

bottles *(never use glass)* with a couple of inches of water frozen in the bottom.

Turns are started by turning the head and shoulders in the direction your child wants to go. The skater should:

• keep their skates about shoulder width apart;

• lead with the inside leg, and start the turn around the marker with the head and shoulders.

Gliding and turning.

Check that their knees are bent, and that they lean slightly inside. Be sure that they practice gentle turns in both directions. Patience is required here. Turning can be quite tricky for the beginner. All that is needed is a little time, and plenty of practice.

From the Basics To...

Now that your child is doing some things on their own you will be more effective if you ask them to, "Watch this—then try it yourself," and then demonstrate the skill yourself, or get someone else to demonstrate. Then let your child have a try. Just be sure that your child has enough control to have a good chance of success after a few tries.

Our explanation of skills is to help you help your child. Information should only be passed along when you think it will help them learn. In many cases, it is more effective to ask them to watch a simple demonstration.

Once the child is confident, and capable of turning on both feet with some degree of control, ask them to try doing it on one foot. Ask them to try gliding on either foot, and then practice turning to the left and then to the right.

Gliding, Sitting and Standing

Here are some fun exercises to develop balance and gliding ability:
- push the skater off in an upright glide (A);
- let them glide for a few moments, and then have them bend at the knees (B);
- ask them to drop their seat an inch or two, in order to assume a slight sitting position for a few moments;
- then return to an upright glide again (C).

Gliding with Skates Different Widths Apart

Ask them to try gliding with the skates shoulder-width apart, then with them as far apart as possible, then with their feet tight together.

Gliding, sitting and standing.

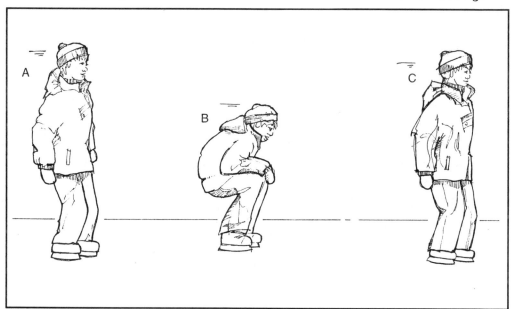

55

Other Activities

Let them try walking across the ice on the toes of their skates, and then back again on the heels.

Remember, all of these activities can be introduced by saying "Watch this—try it yourself," as long as you are quite sure they have developed enough skill so that they have a good chance of being successful after a few tries.

Sculling Forward

Once your child can glide forward on both skates really well, they can try to "scull." Starting in the basic stance, ask your child to:

• turn their feet out (A);

• when they push their feet forward (heels in, toes out) they will start moving forwards (B);

Sculling forward.

• when the feet are about shoulder-width apart ask the

skater to turn the toes in, pull the feet back together again (toes first), and straighten the legs a little (C);

• just before the toes touch, the skater should bend slightly at the knees, turn the toes out and repeat the exercise over and over. Now your child is sculling and skating forward under their own steam!

The skater may want to hold onto something at first— that's fine. A partner can hold the learner's hands, or both of you can hold onto a stick, or the skater can push off from something, glide, and then scull.

Position of the feet when sculling forward, as seen from above.

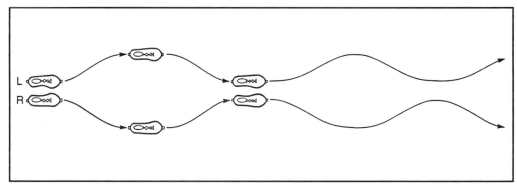

As the skater becomes more proficient, the sculling action will become more powerful.

Be patient—with time, encouragement and practice your skater will learn to scull in a series of fluid, non-stop movements. See how many times they can scull forwards across the ice without falling.

The T-Push and Glide

Once your child can walk, glide and scull on their own on both skates, they can try and put all these skills together. The skater starts by taking three short steps, and then gliding on both feet (step—step—step—glide). Try it again. Now let them try four or five steps, followed by a glide and, as their speed slows, have them make a turn to either right or left. Next, ask them to take a few steps, and then glide on one foot by lifting the other foot up.

They may need a little support to start off with. Soon they'll be able to do it more on their own. They can practice this until they can glide with some control on one foot. Build up to five or six steps and a glide. Can they cross the rink, or glide along its length?

The T-push and glide, starting position.

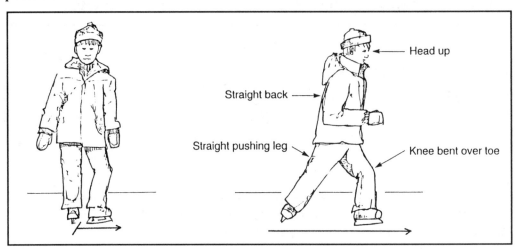

Head up

Straight back

Straight pushing leg

Knee bent over toe

A better way to start off and glide further is to start with the skates in a T, as shown. In this start position:

• the instep of the right skate is set behind the heel of the left;

• the whole blade of the back (right) skate is on the ice;

• the skater uses the arms for balance;

• start with a firm push with the back (right) skate;

• by the end of the push the skater's weight should be shifted onto the front (left) skate, so they are now gliding on one skate;

- make sure they keep the front knee bent (knees over the toe);
- make sure the pushing leg ends fully straightened;
- use gentle pushes at first. The skater can push with more force as their control improves;
- once they get the hang of it with the preferred foot forward, have them try with the other foot forward.
- they can reverse the feet if they are more comfortable with the right foot forward.

The T-push and glide is a key to good skating.

Now the skater can try to stroke around the rink with repeated pushes. Push, glide on the lead foot, push again and glide again. Each time the back skate should be set down at about 90° to the front, and the push ends with the back leg straight. Work on this until your child can do three or four successive pushes with either foot leading.

Stroking

Once they are comfortable with gliding, they can start gently stroking with both skates. Beginning with a T-start, your child can glide on the right skate and bring the left (rear) skate parallel to the front skate, gliding with both feet together. Then they:

- lift the right skate, turn it out to the side, dig the whole blade into the ice, push backwards and glide on the left skate;
- next, bring the right skate forward, placing it parallel to the left skate;
- once they've got their balance, they can push out with the left skate again.

Have them repeat this cycle around the rink, alternating legs—now they're really skating on their own! If they need

Stroking—the T-push and glide.

Playing aeroplane.

a little help balancing, hold onto one of their hands for a while, until they get the hang of it.

Now all they need is some practice. Following are some fun games they can try.

Playing Aeroplane

Take two or three strokes and glide on one skate, with the rear leg extended behind and arms stretched to the side;

• glide for two or three counts and then change the skates over.

Chasing the Ball

Roll a ball about the size of a tennis ball along the ice. Chase it and ask your child to pick it up with the right, left or both hands;

• then they can kick the ball along the ice with either skate, and pick it up with the right, left and then both hands.

Skating Around the Markers

Place some plastic bottles or pylons on the ice in some simple pattern, and have them skate and glide around the course. The course can be easy at first with a few gentle turns, and then made more difficult with the pylons placed closer together. For examples of a course, see the three diagrams on the next page.

As the skater's skill and confidence grow, encourage them to cover the course faster, in both directions.

Skating around the markers.

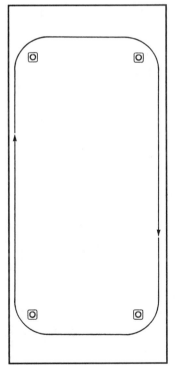 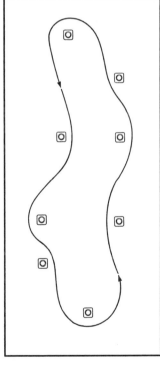 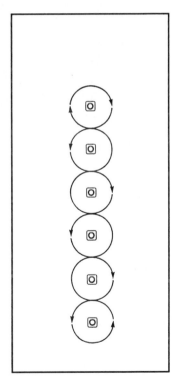

Warming Up and Cooling Down

Now is a good time to teach your skater good "warm-up" and "cool-down" habits, as they are fast becoming able to skate faster and harder.

"Warming up" refers to doing some light exercise to warm up the body. This allows the heart, lungs and muscles to work more efficiently, and it's also thought to help prevent injuries.

To warm up, ask your child to do some slow, easy skating for about five minutes or so before they start their harder skating. They can speed up near the end of the warm-up period.

"Cooling down" refers to a process opposite to warming up. Ask your skater to do some very light skating or walking a few minutes after the main skating session, in order to help the blood return from the legs to the rest of the body. A few light stretches are a good idea, too.

We will not get too technical here. For the more advanced skater, warm-up drills and stretches are described in some of the references in the Further Reading section.

Bob Anderson's *Stretching* book gives some useful ideas for stretches to be done before and after many types of exercise including skating. This book is available in many bookstores or libraries.

6

Stopping

JOEL RUSS

Your child will already have found some simple ways to stop, even if it is only by sitting down on the ice - or through controlled collisions with you or the boards! Now is the time for your skater to learn some of the standard ways to stop.

The Snowplow

One of the easiest ways to stop is the "snowplow." This is done first with either foot (a half snowplow), and then with both feet (a full snowplow).

A half snowplow—feel the skate blade on the ice!

To do the half snowplow:

• first, so your child can get the feeling for this while standing or holding onto something, ask them to turn their left skate toe in with the heel out;

• then, push the skate forward with the *inside* edge of the skate scraping across the ice, as in the illustration.

See if they can build up a little ridge of snow by doing this several times. Next, try it with the right foot. Can they feel the resistance of the ice as the blade scrapes forward?

Now, ask your skater to try it while they're scooting:

• have them push forward and glide;

64

• then ask them to try to place their left foot in front, and plow along the ice to stop;

• now have them try it with the right foot.

Practice each of these. Once they have some control in using either foot for stopping, they can now try a full snowplow with *both* feet.

A full snowplow.

While gliding forward, ask them to try turning both toes in and heels out. The skater should try to *push hard* sideways on both skates, and dig in using the inside edges of both blades.

Have them practice this until they can stop with confidence, and without falling down. Encourage them to keep their body upright, with a slight bend of the knees, and to keep travelling straight while coming to a stop. Following are some start and stop games to help their practice:

Freeze Tag

With a group of friends, one player is "it" and the others try not to be tagged. A player can only be safe from being tagged if they are motionless. If the person who is "it" tags a player before they can stop and "freeze", the tagged player becomes it.

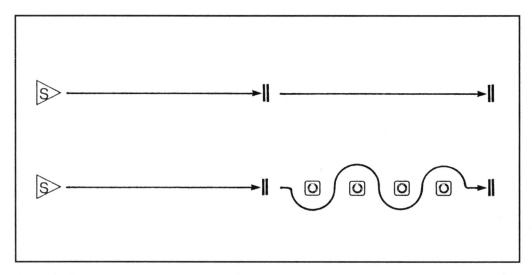

Start and stop games: starting, gliding and stopping (top); starting, glide turning and stopping (bottom).

Obstacle Course

See the example of an obstacle course shown on the next page. The skaters should:
- skate up to the obstacles;
- step over wooden planks or hockey sticks;
- glide or scoot around the pylons;
- dive under the pylons, get up;
- glide turn;
- jump from one or both feet over the stick;
- then stop.

Catch-up

The skater can give someone a long lead, and then try to catch up to them. Combine this game with the obstacle course for an added challenge and more fun.

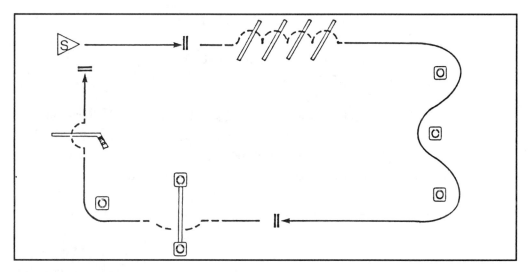

The Hockey Stop

An example of an obstacle course.

The most efficient way to stop is by using *both* feet as brakes, as in the illustration on page 6. This is known as the "hockey stop."

In this manoeuvre, the feet are turned 90 degrees to the skating direction, resulting in a stop. The turn can be performed either to the left or right.

A right sided turn is described here. Just do the opposite to turn to the left.

As with most of these exercises, get your child to start gliding in the basic stance, feet shoulder-width apart.

They can get their skates to turn sideways by turning their shoulders to the right. The hips will follow.

Then the skater can turn both skates perpendicular to the skating direction.

As they do this make sure they lean well back, and bend their knees as they turn.

The skater will scrape or skid across the ice on the *inside* edge of the front skate and on the *outside* edge of the rear skate.

As they slow down, make sure they keep their skates about shoulder-width apart, with the weight shared equally on both skates.

Finally, as they brake, they should extend their front leg.

At first the skater should turn to whichever side they prefer. Once they get the hang of it, they can start practicing stopping both ways, to the right and to the left.

This is a skill to try slowly at first. As your child gains more confidence, they can try doing it when they skate faster. As when learning the other skills, they may want to hold onto someone or something at first to help their balance.

Remember—practice makes perfect. On the next page are some ideas to help them practice and improve.

The hockey stop.

Skate/Stop/Skate

Have them alternate skating and stopping as they go down the ice.

Reversing the Directions

Perform a hockey stop;
- then make a T, with the front skate facing forward and the rear foot forming the bar of the T (see the section on the T Start);
- perform a T-start in the opposite direction;
- then stride away;
- go up and down the ice practicing this.

Reversing the directions.

7
Forward Striding

JOEL RUSS

The V-Start

Now your child can stroke and stop. The next thing for them to learn is to put more power and speed into their skating stride and starts. The V-start is the best way of achieving both these goals.

From the basic stance, the skater should:
- turn their feet out into a V;
- lean forward slightly;
- this start is more like a run, with the first strides being very short, and becoming longer as the skater gains speed.

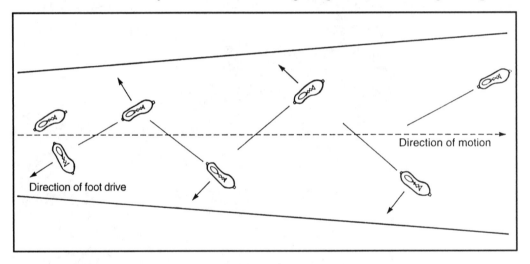

Direction of motion

Direction of foot drive

Skate position in front starts.

The first drive is like a T-start with the rear skate (left or right) set at about 90° to the front skate. Your child should learn to drive off with either skate.

The second drive is with the opposite skate, pushing out to the side. The angle of the skate's blade will be a little less than 45° after the third or fourth stride. As the skater speeds up, the angle between the skate and the line of direction becomes less.

From then on the skating stride should be an alternating series of pushes and glides, with the blade of the skate turned out a bit less than 45°. Each push is followed by a glide on the opposite skate. During the glide, the driving leg is brought forward close to the gliding leg, with the skate close to the ice. As the skate returns to the ice the skater's body leans forward, so that the weight is taken on that leg just as the next stroke or push begins.

Pushing and gliding.

As your child's skating speed increases they will take fewer strides to maintain speed, and they will be standing more upright. It will soon be possible for them to establish an easy and even skating rhythm.

Pushing and Gliding

To gain more speed your child should push their leg out so that it is extended from the hip to the toe. After pushing, all of the weight will be on the forward (gliding) foot.

Remember that to gain speed your child will take fast, short strides. Once speed is developed the skater may glide longer, taking fewer strides.

Once your young skater is able to start, stop, turn, and get up some speed, they can do more games and practice so that improvement comes more rapidly.

*The push and
glide sequence.*

Here are some games you might like to try:

Race
Race a friend down the ice (and back).

Rope or Stick-pull
Use a stick or a piece of rope to pull a friend around the rink.

Dodge the Ball
Play Dodge the Ball on skates:
   • the one who is "it" tries to hit another player with a light ball (e.g., a foam ball);
   • when they succeed, the hit person becomes "it".

Relay
Skate around a pylon and back, and tag a friend; now it's their turn to go.
 • if there are enough people, make two teams—who's the first to finish?

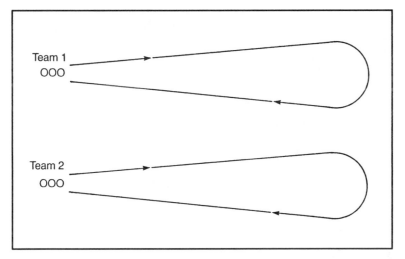

Team relay.

Speed-ups
Put a pylon twenty feet down the ice. Ask your child to start slowly, and then accelerate by doing quick strides as they reach the marker.

Speed changes
Ask your child to skate, stop and turn around:
 • have them accelerate in the opposite direction;
 • finally, ask them to try and run across the ice on their skates.

What other games can you think of...or make up?

8

Skating Backwards

JOEL RUSS

Stopping while skating backwards is described at the end of this chapter since it is the most difficult skill. Usually, when learning to skate backwards, young children just glide to a halt, or perhaps fall down.

Stance for skating backwards.

Skating backwards is important if one wants to be really good on skates. It is quite hard for most people at first.

This is another case where a little bit of instruction is all that's needed. Success will follow if there is a lot of encouragement and plenty of practice.

There are two complications in learning to skate backwards:

1) you can't see where you are going and this makes one a little nervous (how often do we walk backwards?), and

2) falling when skating backwards is a little more possible and dangerous because of this.

So, first get your child used to going backwards on skates by asking them to walk backwards. Holding one or both of their hands, or using a chair or the rink boards to hold onto may help them overcome their nervousness.

Gradually, over ten to twenty practice sessions of five to ten minutes each, your child will gain confidence and begin to get some control.

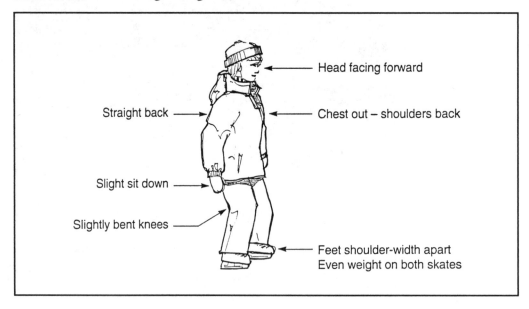

Head facing forward

Straight back

Chest out – shoulders back

Slight sit down

Slightly bent knees

Feet shoulder-width apart
Even weight on both skates

Beginning Steps

In the beginning, have your child walk backwards a bit pigeon-toed (toes facing in, heels apart); and ask them to walk across the rink four or five times.

Encourage them by sharing in their excitement, praising both their willingness to try and their early success in being able to take two or three, then four or five steps backwards without falling. Some fun exercises for your child to do while learning to glide backwards follow.

Pushing off and gliding backwards.

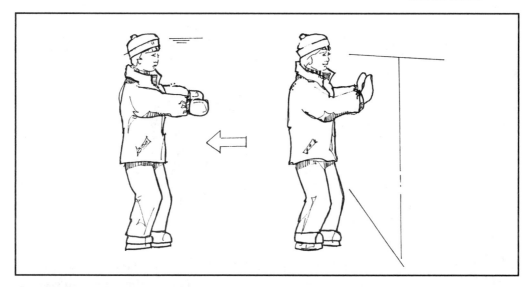

Coasting Backwards

The skater can push against something (or somebody) and try to glide slowly backwards—very slowly at first—on both skates.

Coasting Backwards for Distance

Your child might also want to play a game with a friend, to

79

see who can glide furthest. How far can they glide? Make a mark on the ice and see if they can beat it!

You or a partner could skate forward and push your child gently backwards, while they glide, then trade places. You can both do this with hockey or broom sticks between you.

When they feel ready, let them try gliding backwards on *one* skate. Once again, they can try it with a partner holding onto them.

Gliding backwards with sticks.

At first, only practice on the leg that the child feels more secure on. Later have them practice on the other leg so they get good on both feet. Once they can glide backwards really well, they could try to scull backwards.

Sculling Backwards

To scull, your child should:
- start in the backward stance, but with feet turned in;
- next, ask them to push their feet apart, and their heels

out. This will start them moving backwards;

• when their feet are comfortably apart (shoulder width), ask them to pull them back together, heels first and knees straight;

• just before the heels touch, ask your child to turn their toes in, their heels out and to bend their knees again.

When they repeat this exercise over and over, they'll be sculling and skating backwards! Again, if they want to hold onto someone in the early stages, let them. They can try sculling with a partner holding hands, or with sticks. The beginning backwards skater can push off from someone, or from the boards (if there are any), glide, and then start to scull backwards.

As your young skater gets better, the sculling action will become more powerful. Then they can try to *pull* their partner while they glide.

Backwards sculling.

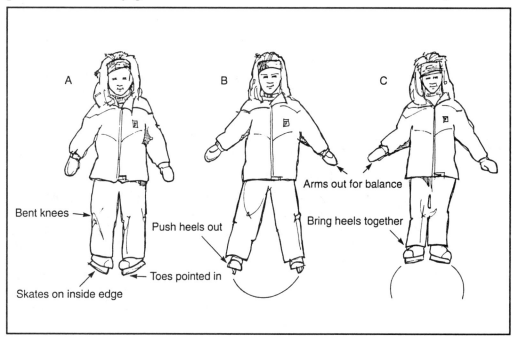

This will take a lot of encouragement and practice, but the stage where they can scull backwards on their own in a series of fluid, non-stop movements will eventually come. Your patience will be as important during this process as their own. How many times can they go the length of the ice forward and backwards without falling?

Once they can scull and glide with both feet, they can try it with one foot by lifting one of their feet off the ice (lift and glide). This is really hard!

Starting Backwards — The C-cut

The C-cut is the most efficient stroke for starting backwards. The C-cut is a semi-circle on the ice with one skate, while the other moves straight back.

As with sculling, the skater should:

- start with the toes pointed in;
- press on the ball of the right foot (A);
- push down and straighten the leg (B);
- and make a semi-circle on the ice.

Initially the weight should be on the pushing (driving) leg (here it's the right), but as the right leg goes out to the side, the skater should transfer their weight to the left skate. As they return the right leg (C), the skater should bring it in parallel to the left skate. This action is then repeated using the other foot.

Initially your child can try the C-cut while standing.

Ask them to try cutting semi-circles on the ice with each foot. If they wish, they can hold onto a partner, a chair or the boards to start.

Your child can practice doing C-cuts across the rink with one leg driving, and then return with the other leg driving. Eventually they will be able to alternate feet, but in the

early stages allow them to concentrate on a preferred foot. *The C-cut.*

Your child might try starting with C-cuts, and then scull backwards. Once they can scull backwards, do C-cuts on both feet *and* glide backwards on one foot, they are ready to stroke backwards.

Stroking Backwards

Ask your skater to get up some momentum by C-cutting or sculling backwards, and then ask them to glide, with their feet parallel. Once they're gliding they should turn their right skate toe-in, and push it out forward and to the right side, gliding back on the left skate.

When they finish pushing with the right skate, they shift their weight onto the left skate and they lift the right skate from the ice bringing it parallel to the left skate. Repeat the movement pushing with the right skate, gliding on the left.

Have them try to cross the ice with as few strokes as possible. Once they reach the other side, ask them to return by pushing with the left skate and gliding on the right.

When your child is able to cross the rink a few times using each foot, they can start using alternate strokes. Have

The sequence for backwards striding is shown going from left to right.

them scull backwards, glide with their feet parallel, push back with one skate and glide on the other. Then bring the feet together and glide backwards with both feet.

They can progress to gliding on one foot, and as the driving foot comes back parallel to the gliding foot, the skater drops the driving foot back onto the ice, and pushes off with the other foot—left-push, glide, right-push, glide.

Stopping while Skating Backwards

The easiest way to stop when skating backwards is the backwards snowplow or V-stop:

• as the skater glides backwards on both feet, they bend their knees;

• turn the toes of both feet out (heels in);

• straighten the legs, exerting pressure on the ice with the inside edges of both skates.

Your child can practice by gently pushing away

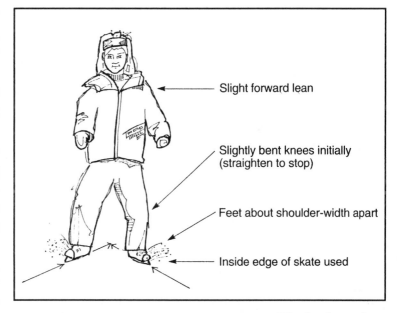

Slight forward lean

Slightly bent knees initially (straighten to stop)

Feet about shoulder-width apart

Inside edge of skate used

The backwards V-stop.

from an object or a partner and practicing the stop. A partner can push the other skater backwards while they try to resist, using the snow-plow stop skate position. Partners should change over when they reach the end of the rink.

Here are more games to practice backward skating:

Backwards Tag

Once your child can skate backwards really well, they can begin to play tag skating backwards. Make sure everybody looks back often to see where they're going!

Big Circle

Skate backwards in a big circle through a series of pylons. At first make it easy with a few pylons and gentle turns (e.g. a square). Later you can add more pylons.

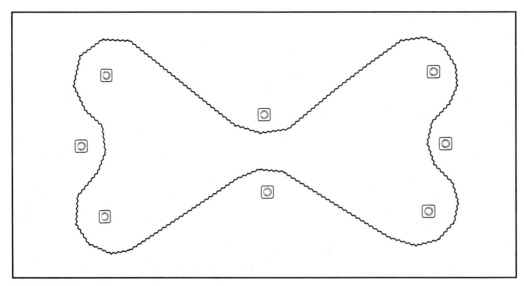

Backwards skating—a big circle.

Zig-zag.

Zig-zag

Skate forward and backwards across the ice in a zig-zag pattern (set the course up with pylons).

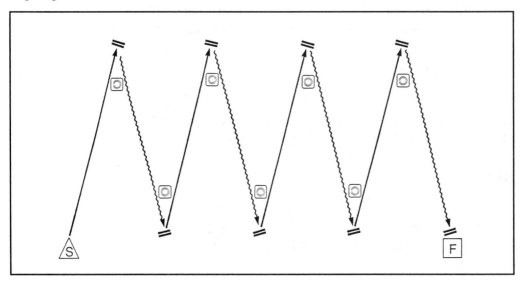

9
Turning and Edge Control

Over to You

From this point on, to simplify things we'll describe the skills so that you can teach yourself—or review them if they are familiar to you—and then you can pass them on to your child in the best way you see fit.

Try to follow the instructions, gain some reasonable skill, and then help your young learner to learn them.

Remember how effective a simple demonstration with only minimal explanation can be—"Watch this, now you try it."

Skate Edges

Each skate is "hollow ground" by the skate sharpening machine to leave two edges on the skate blade—an inside edge and an outside edge.

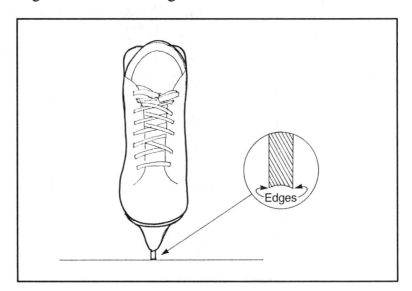

The "hollow ground" skate.

While standing erect and gliding straight along the ice, both edges cut into the ice evenly.

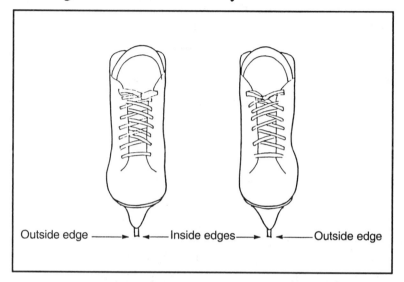

Outside edge ⟶ ⟵ Inside edges ⟶ ⟵ Outside edge

Blade position on upright skates.

When turning and leaning to the right, the lean shifts the weight to the outside edge of the right skate and the inside edge of the left.

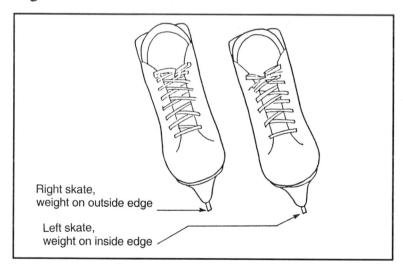

Right skate, weight on outside edge

Left skate, weight on inside edge

Skate blade position when turning.

The best way to become aware of your skate edge is to glide around a curve. Try coasting or gliding around long curves on both skates at first, and then you can try it on one skate.

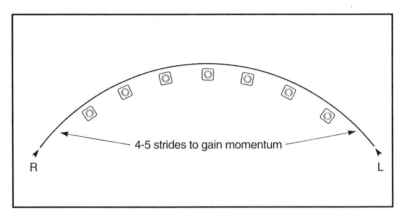

4-5 strides to gain momentum

R   L

Skating on a curve.

Be sure to practice skating in both directions around curves, first on both skates, and then on either skate.

You can practice this with a gentle weaving motion or in a slalom. Again, once you can do it with both skates, try gliding on one skate.

Scooting

A good way to practice is to "scoot" in a circle. Scooting is what you do when you put one foot on a skateboard and

Gliding and turning.

90

TURNING AND EDGE CONTROL

pump or scoot yourself along by pushing off the sidewalk
or road with the other foot.

You can practice scooting in a couple of ways:

• circle to your left, and coast or glide on your left skate
while you push or scoot yourself along with the right skate;

• while circling to your right, coast or glide on your
right skate while scooting with your left.

In each case, the weight on the gliding skate is mostly on
the outside edge while you scoot off of the inside edge of
the pumping skate.

Scooting counter-clockwise and clockwise.

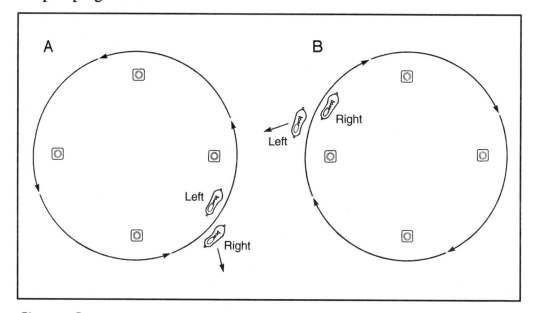

Cross-Overs

From gliding in a circle you can progress to continuous
skating in a circle by learning cross-overs.

Cross-overs allow a skater to maintain greater speed and
even accelerate while circling. Without cross-overs a
skater can only coast or glide around corners.

As with other skating skills, if you learn and practice them without carrying a hockey stick you'll be a much better skater in the long run.

To learn the cross-over action review scooting in a circle a couple of times. Select the circle direction, to your right or left, that feels most natural to you.

Begin cross-overs going in your preferred direction. We will describe circling to the left; you should reverse the description if you prefer going to your right.

• begin a new circle to the left, coasting on your left skate;

• make a single scooting action with your right skate;

• as you lift the right skate up, cross it over in front of your left skate to place it on the ice in front of, and about parallel to, the left one.

Your legs will be crossed for a moment. As your weight shifts onto your right skate, bring your left skate forward to continue in the circle. Now you are ready to scoot and cross over again. You're away!

Keep practicing in your preferred direction until you are able to cross-over continuously in a circle three or four times without falling. When you can do that start practicing in the opposite direction.

At first it is easier to push with the outside skate and glide on the inside skate: *stroke right—glide left, cross right over left, stroke right—glide left.*

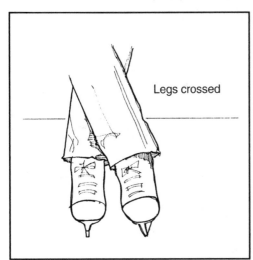

Foot position in cross-over stride.

Make sure you can do it in both directions. Once you are confident pushing with the outside foot, push off with the inside foot too.

Following are ways to help learn the crossing over action. Do all the exercises without a stick or puck at first, until you are confident you can perform the skill well. Then try them with a stick or puck.

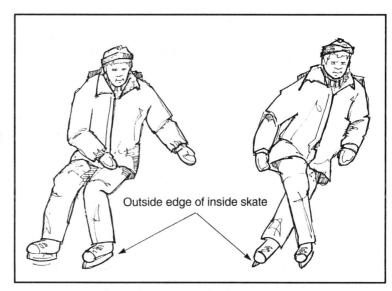

Outside edge of inside skate

Circles

Practice skating in circles in both directions. Begin with large circles; as you get better, practice going very fast and skating in smaller circles.

A different view of the cross-over.

Figure-8.

Figure-8

Skate in a Figure-8 on the ice. This requires you to practice cross-overs in both directions. Try doing the figure-8s in larger and smaller circles. Try to make the turns tighter as you improve.

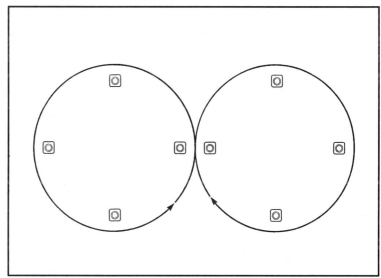

Train

Do cross-overs in both directions around the rink with friends while holding onto a piece of rope to form a "train."

Weaving or Slalom

This involves skating in between markers as we have explained in previous chapters. This time, however, do cross-overs as you go around the markers.

Circle Tag

Form a large circle with a number of friends. Each player takes a turn at being a tagger and a chaser:
- tagger (1) skates on the outside of the circle, and touches another skater (2) on the back;
- the tagger skates around the circle with (2) in pursuit;
- tagger tries to get into (2)'s spot without being touched;
- everyone has a turn;
- switch your direction;
- make sure everyone uses forward cross-overs.

If you're cold, have everyone skate slowly in a circle while the chase is going on outside the group.

Circle tag.

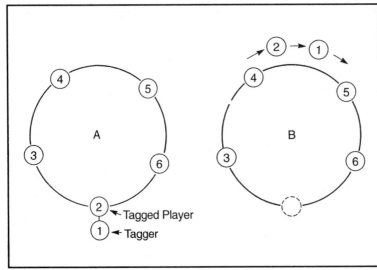

94

Sharper Turns

Lean into the turn; turn around a friend or a marker, trying to increase the sharpness of the turn.

Guess the Direction

Skate towards a friend, and when you're about six feet away, they should indicate which way you turn (left or right);
- use strong cross-over strides to make your turn;
- you'll have to be evenly balanced because you won't know which way you'll have to turn;
- try to accelerate around turns and not lose any speed—at first this will not be possible, but keep working on it.

10
Intermediate Skating Skills

Pivoting

A pivot is a quick rotation to face the opposite direction. There are two basic pivots to learn—the forward standing pivot, and the backward pivot.

Your long range goal is to be able to do a controlled pivot, without a stick, forward to backward, and backward to forward, turning *either* to the right or left. When you have learned these four variations you will be well on your way to being a top-notch skater!

One has to be able to skate backwards quite well before learning to do a pivot. It will help you to practice some more backward skating before starting on pivoting.

Begin with whichever one you prefer, forward or backward. Once you can do the easier one quite well, begin to work on the other one. For best results learn pivoting without carrying a stick.

In a forward or backward pivot you can pivot (or turn) either to your right or left. Again, begin with whichever one you prefer, and the one that feels best for you. Once you can do that one, then switch directions.

It will take you at least a couple of winters before you are able do all four pivot variations smoothly and at your top speed. It won't happen in a couple of weeks!

Be patient and keep working, and as you gain control over each one, go on to the next one. Some will be easier than others, but with persistent practice all four will feel natural to you before long.

Don't hurry, be patient. Pick away at it and give yourself time. Be sure to wait until you are good at pivoting in your preferred direction before you start to practice the pivot to the opposite side.

Now let's see how to do a good pivot. Since a lot of beginning skaters find it easier to do a forward pivot, that's the one we'll describe first.

Standing Forward Pivot

For a simple start:

• stand still in your basic stance, blades parallel and about shoulder width apart, slight lean forward, slight bend in your knees;

• turn around with a kind of shuffling action to face the opposite direction—you'll probably fall down!

Try it turning to both right and left to see which one is easier for you. Practice the easier one until you can do two or three in a row without falling down. Don't rush it.

When you can keep standing after you've shuffled your way around, try the following to make it more like a real pivot:

The standing forward pivot (to the left).

To turn to the right (reverse these directions for left pivot):

• twist your upper body a bit to the right;
• as you do, lift up your right skate and turn your foot to place the skate on the ice so it points as close as you can get it in the opposite direction;
• as your right leg swings around, let your left skate twist a bit in the same direction;
• transfer the weight to your right skate;
• lift your left skate and swing it around parallel to your right skate.

You'll probably fall down again! Everybody does. Keep at it, though—you'll soon get the feel of it.

Some helpful hints to remember when learning the forward standing pivot:

• don't try to master it in one day;
• do it 10 or 15 times and then go on to having fun or trying other things you're learning to do;
• come back to practicing pivoting later in the same session or the next time you're on the ice;
• sometimes you'll find that if you leave it alone for a while, the next time you practice you'll do much better. The key is going back to it regularly until that happens.

When you've got the standard pivot down well enough that you can do three or four in a row without falling, go on to practicing it while moving.

Forward Pivot—Moving

Pivot in the direction that's easier for you. We'll describe a pivot to the left, but you can reverse it for a right pivot:

• start skating backward, not too fast;
• glide in your basic stance (with blades parallel, about

shoulder width apart, slight lean and knees bent);
* when you're ready, shift your weight to your right skate as you twist your left shoulder back;
* lift your left skate and swing it around to point in the opposite direction;
* then put your weight on the left skate and swing your right skate around to complete the pivot;
* glide for a moment to keep your balance.

Player glides backwards
Weight on right skate

Transfer the weight to
left skate, dig in
right skate and push

Direction of movement

Helpful hints when learning the forward moving pivot:
* once you get used to it, accelerate out of the turn by striding hard with your right foot just before it leaves the ice;

The forward pivot while moving.

• try to increase your backwards skating speed;

• see if you can stay on the same straight line after pivoting without veering off to either side.

When you are quite good at your preferred turn, whether it is to the left or right, begin to work on the opposite turn.

Direction of movement

The backward pivot while moving.

Backward Pivot—Moving

In the backwards pivot you skate forward, then pivot backwards 180° so that you keep going in the same direction, but now you are facing backwards.

You begin by skating forward and then pivot to backwards skating. The pivot to your right is described below. Reverse the action if you prefer to begin with the pivot to your left. The sequence of actions is:

• your weight is on your left skate;

• lift your right skate;

- twist your right shoulder backwards and place your right skate 180° to your left skate—heel to heel;
  - the weight shifts from the left skate to the right skate;
  - place your left skate parallel to the right skate and begin to skate backwards.

When you are good at this pivot to your preferred side, begin to work on the other side. As you gain control, speed up before the pivot and to accelerate after it by pushing off with your skates, until you can do it at your top speed.

Here are some ways to practice your pivots:

- start at the end of the rink and stride forward, do a left backward pivot, speed up as you go backwards, do a left forward pivot and come out of it striding hard;
- return the same way, but this time pivot to your right both times;
- return with a left backward pivot and a right forward pivot;
- start skating backwards and do a left forward pivot, stride hard coming out of it, then do a left backward pivot;
- start backwards, do both right pivots;
- start backwards, do a left forward followed by a right backward pivot.

Build up this list of different ways to pivot over many months. Be patient. All this practice will pay off in greater skating enjoyment, and in more effective hockey for those who want to improve their playing ability.

Moving Sideways

This is a good way to improve balance, agility and the basic movement of crossing over, which is essential in skillful skating.

Try to walk sideways across the ice (like a crab). Your

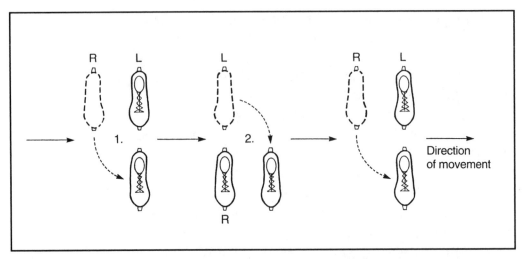

Foot positions for moving sideways to the right (as seen from above).

body keeps facing forward, shoulders square and skates are placed flat on the ice. As usual, try this slowly at first and as you get the feel of it speed up a bit. Practice moving to the left or right, whichever feels better for you.

If you want to move to the left, start in the basic stance, facing forward, and:
- place right foot in front of the left, facing forward;
- swing the left foot behind the right foot and place it in the basic stance position again;
- reverse the action if you want to move to the right;
- continue this process until you reach the other side of the ice;
- return leading with the other foot.

When you can do this well you can try something a bit more advanced, again moving to the left. This time *cross* your skates over so that the right skate crosses over in front of the left skate, and is placed outside the left skate.

Your skates are now crossed over. The left skate is now swung behind the right skate, and placed beside it to return to the basic stance with the skates parallel.

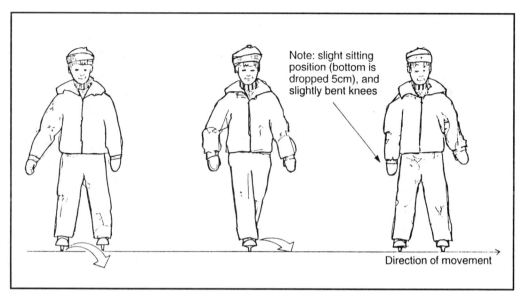

Note: slight sitting position (bottom is dropped 5cm), and slightly bent knees

Direction of movement

To move right the actions are reversed: the left skate crosses over in front of the right skate, and the right skate swings *behind* the left skate.

Practice this without a stick until you can do it smoothly and under control, both left and right, all the way across the rink. When you use a stick make sure you keep it well out

Moving sideways as viewed from the front.

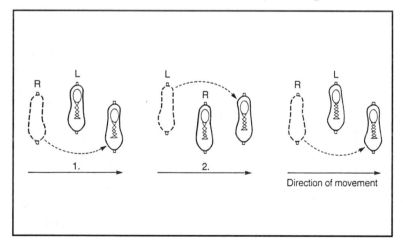

1.　2.

Direction of movement

Foot positions for moving sideways (to right) with cross-overs.

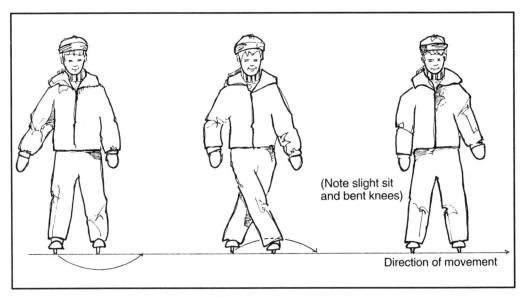

(Note slight sit and bent knees)

Direction of movement

Moving sideways with cross-overs as seen from the front.

in front of you, with the blade on the ice. Don't carry the stick parallel to the ice with the blade pointing upwards and off the ice, where you couldn't receive a pass.

Here are drills to help you practice moving sideways. Do these drills *without* a stick until you can do them at top speed without falling:

Facing this direction

Moving sideways exercise.

• side-step across the rink to the right and then return to the left;

• start two or three strides forward, hockey stop, then side-step across the

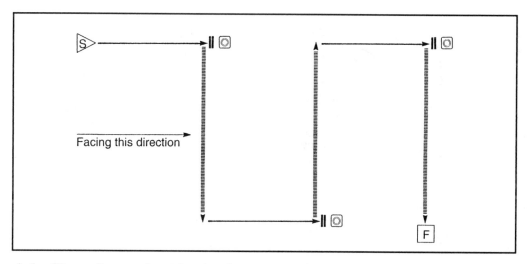

Facing this direction

rink. Skate forward again, hockey stop, sidestep back across the ice. Repeat all the way down the rink. Always face down the rink, and don't turn your back on the direction you're going.

More exercises (above and below) for moving sideways.

• sidestep to the right across the rink, skate backwards to the other end, sidestep to the left back across the rink again, push off and stride forward as fast as you can,

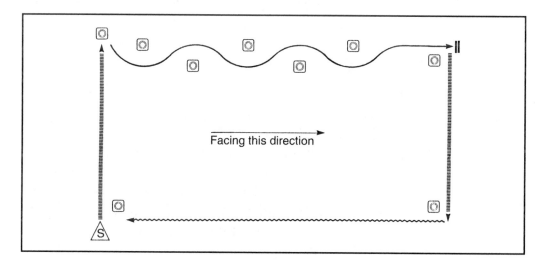

Facing this direction

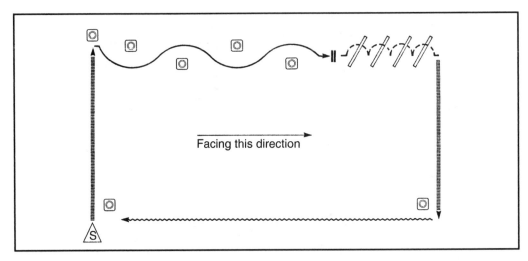

Facing this direction

An additional exercise for moving sideways.

hockey stop at the end. Reverse the direction next time;

• sidestep to the left across the rink, stride forward and weave through the markers, sidestep right across the rink, skate backwards as fast as you can, do a backwards stop. Reverse the directions next time.

• sidestep left across the rink, stride forward and weave through the markers, step-jump over some sticks (3 feet long) lying on the ice, sidestep to the right across the rink, skate backwards as fast as you can. Reverse the direction.

Timing Your Drills

Have someone time you with a stopwatch or the sweep second hand of a watch after you get used to these drills. Time yourself skating in both directions. If you are slower going in one direction, practice that one more until your times in each direction are close. Always set the markers and sticks in the same place each time so you can time yourself over the same distance. Keep a record of your times so you can see your improvement.

Tight Turns

Once you can control your balance while skating fairly fast, you can start to learn tight turns. These allow you to change direction very quickly without wasting very much of your speed.

If you don't carry a stick while you learn tight turns, you'll develop much better balance and be a more skillful skater and puck-handler when you do add the stick.

Lead up to tight turning by:

- skating towards a marker;
- coasting around it in a fairly wide circle;
- keeping your knees bent and the skates parallel at first.

As you get better, make the arc smaller as you circle around the marker. Practice turning to both right and left by using two markers and doing a Figure-8 around them.

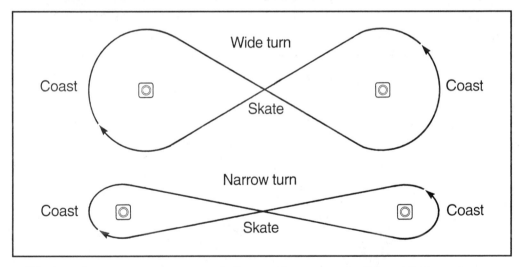

Notice that as you go around the marker, your inside skate tends to slide ahead of the other skate. It helps if you lean slightly in the direction of the turn.

Wide and narrow turns.

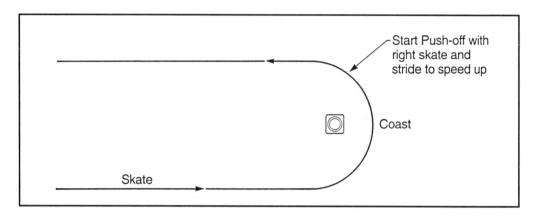

Start Push-off with right skate and stride to speed up

Coast

Skate

A tight turn to the left.

As you get better at this kind of turn, speed up and start the turn by turning your head and shoulders in the direction you want to turn. Slide the left skate ahead of the right skate as you turn left, and vice-versa as you turn right.

Pushing off as you complete the turn.

Once you've got the hang of it, start pushing off with your back foot as soon as you have completed the 180° turn.

A

B

Here are some exercises to help practice turning:

Tandem

Do this one in pairs. While the rear skater pushes, the front skater glides along and tries to change direction with sharp, sudden turns.

Turning Around A Friend

While your friend stands still and has a rest, you skate towards them and turn sharply around them; switch over. Try to get as close as you can without touching.

Timed Turns

Set up two markers and time yourself doing five Figure-8s around them. Keep track of your improvement in speed.

When you can't improve your speed anymore, increase the number of Figure-8s to ten.

Relays

Set up a team of three or four, and place a marker at the end of the rink or 30-60 feet away.

• player one skates hard to the marker and turns around it as sharply as possible, and then returns to the start and tags player two;

• player two then repeats the sequence;

• if you have enough room and enough players you can have a race between two teams.

Which team will be the first to complete the course?

The Backward T-Stop

Ask your child to glide backwards in the basic stance, then have them shift their weight to the right skate;

• swing the left leg back, and plant the left skate at a position 90° to the direction of travel;

• the body then rotates 90° to the left, and the left leg bends as the weight is transferred onto the rear (left) foot;

• the left skate provides the most resistance as it scrapes along the ice on its inside edge;

• the right skate is turned 90° to the left skate in preparation for a T-push start.

Your young skater should begin by turning to the side that feels better for them. Once they get good at it, have them practice doing it to the other side. They should try the T-stop slowly at first.

So far we have shown you some of the basics needed to become a skilled skater. For those interested in hockey, it's time to look at ways of improving puckhandling skills.

The backward T-stop.

11

Basic Puckhandling Skills

Skillful skating and body control set the stage for skillful puckhandling. For the first three or four years youngsters should spend at least half of their time on skates without a stick.

While the stick is very attractive and fun to use, it interferes with the development of skating skills and body control. Later on, when playing hockey, the stick will always be available to pass, receive, shoot or check, since it will never have to be used for helping to control a player's balance.

The Basic Puckhandling Position

The basic puckhandling stance is shown in the illustration below.

Hand position and basic puckhandling stance.

The top hand guides and controls the stick, and should be placed on the top of the stick. The lower hand should be placed 8-12 inches down the shaft. Hold the stick whichever way feels more natural.

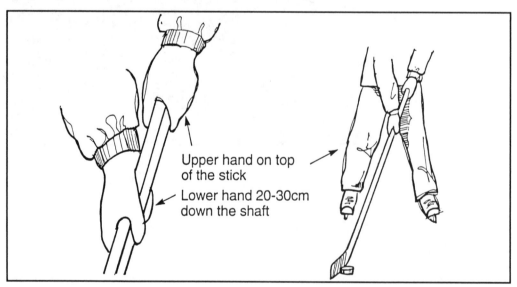

Upper hand on top of the stick

Lower hand 20-30cm down the shaft

Stationary Puckhandling

In the beginning, every youngster wants to watch the puck. Once they are skillful, they can control it by feel, but this will take a lot of time and practice.

The simplest way to learn how to handle and feel the puck is to start by moving the puck on the stick while you are standing still.

Move the puck from side to side by turning over, or rolling the wrists. Try to keep the puck near the centre of the stick blade.

The bottom of the stick blade should be flat on the ice.

Rolling the wrists involves turning the toe of the blade inwards and the heel of the blade outwards.

Practice this first with just the stick in front of you, and then practice it so the tip of the blade touches the ice on either side of the puck.

Now try moving the puck from side to side, cupping or cradling the puck with the stick. This allows more control over the puck.

Try to strive for a smooth and quiet action. At first look down at the puck to see where it is. How many times can you cross the puck in front of you without losing control of it? Try to build up the number. When you can control the puck very well, try looking up every now and then to get the feel of the puck on the stick. Don't force it. Look as long as you need to at first. When you get very good at it, try to close your eyes as you handle the puck. Start with small movements, and then build up the width of the puck

Cupping or cradling the puck.

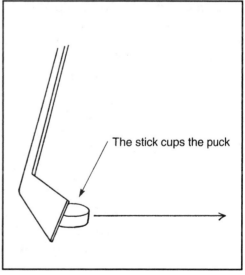

The stick cups the puck

115

movements so they are more than shoulder-width apart. Ideally, you want to be able to control the puck with movements of any width.

Puckhandling stance and stationary puckhandling.

An Important Note about Puck Control

With experience you can begin to lift your head, so that the puck is just visible in the lower edge of the field of vision.

With still more practice you can lift your head and eyes, so that the puck is not seen for a few moments.

Gradually, your child will be able to control the puck by glancing at it every now and then.

Finally, they will be able to control the puck just by the feel of it on their stick.

But to start off with, let your child focus on the puck, just as the beginning piano player focuses on the keys. The process is gradual and cannot be avoided.

It is a mistake to try to get children to handle the puck

without looking at it when they just start, even though many experienced hockey coaches would disagree. The difficulty with such coaches is they know quite a bit about how skilled players operate, but not enough about how people learn complex skills.

Skating Forward with the Puck

When you are familiar with the stationary exercise, you can try to skate with the puck. Here are some points to help you:

• keep the puck well out in front of you, as this helps you to look up;

• keep the puck about the middle of your stick blade, and make sure that the puck always touches the stick;

• at first push the puck on your forehand only (the stick will be to the left of your body if you shoot left—on the right if you shoot right);

• keep both hands on the stick and try to look up as often as you can;

• try to move in a straight line up and down the ice;

• remember to cup the puck by tilting the blade over it—try using the back of your stick, too!

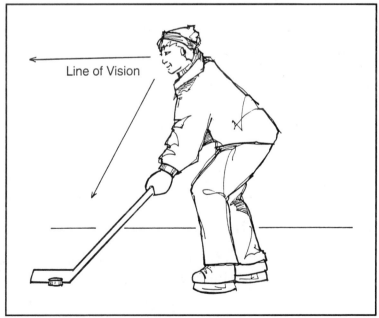

Skating with the puck.

Line of Vision

117

When you can skate with the puck on your backhand and forehand up and down the ice a few (three or four) times without losing it, you can start dribbling the puck. This means moving the puck from side to side in front of you as you skate forward. At first use only the front of the stick, and then the back.

Now that you have learned the basics of skating with the puck, here are some games and exercises you can do on your own or in a group to practice the skills:

Random Skating

Skate all over the rink in any direction. Go as fast or as slow as you like as you control the puck with your stick.

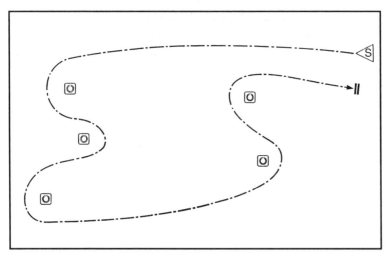

Weaving with the puck.

Weaving with the Puck

Set up markers and weave in between them. Set the markers far apart, making it easier. As the skater gets better, add more markers and set them closer together.

Retrieving a Stationary Puck

Skate past a stationary puck or ball on the ice and try to take it with you as you go by.

Starting with the Puck

Stand still with the puck on your stick. Accelerate into a quick start taking the puck with you.

Skating Backwards with the Puck

This is very similar to skating forward with the puck. Skate backwards with the puck in front of you, and *drag* the puck backwards. Remember to keep the puck cupped with the stick.

Here are some other games to practice puck control:

Keepaway

Play with a friend or partner. Try to keep the puck away from them for as long as possible. Add some more players when you get good at it.

Zig-zagging forward and backward with the puck.

Zig-zag

This is a fun exercise to help practice forward and backwards:

• place cones in the positions shown in the illustration;

• skate backwards to the first cone, then forward to the next,

backwards to the next, and so on.

119

You can place the cones in any position, and alternate forward and backwards skating.

Pig in the Middle

Here is the ice version of this popular game:
- try to keep the puck away from one of your friends ("the pig") while you pass it among yourselves;
- the pig must intercept the pass to stop the game;
- the player whose pass was intercepted then becomes the pig;
- be fair and change around often enough to give everyone a turn.

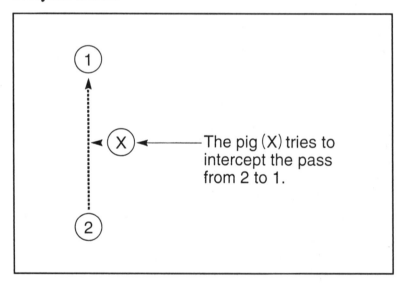

The pig (X) tries to intercept the pass from 2 to 1.

Pig in the middle.

Stopping with the puck

You can try stopping with the puck either with a snow-plow stop, or with a two-foot hockey stop. Try to control the puck by cupping or cradling it with your stick.

Be sure you can do the stop *without* a stick or puck before you try it with a stick or puck. Here is a good example of where players use the stick to help balance when it should be used only to control the puck!

Here are some exercises to help you practice stopping with the puck:

• at the beginning, practice stopping with the puck gently, and then you can pick up speed;

Cradle the Puck

A snowplow stop with the puck.

• try skating with the puck down the rink, *stop* at the other end, turn around and skate back to the start;

• as you improve, speed up, stop and start back as fast as you can.

If you have some friends with you, form equal teams and have a relay if you want some friendly competition. See which team can get all their players to take a puck down the ice and back. If a team has one less skater, have the first skater go both first and last on their team. Another variation is to go forward one way, and backwards the other way.

Be inventive and have some fun!

12

Passing and Receiving

The sweep shot and passing are very similar skills. The easiest way to learn to do both is to start from a stationary position, passing the puck or ball towards a target.

Stationary Forehand Passing and Shooting

The forehand pass is a sweeping motion with the stick, taken from the basic stickhandling position. Here's how to do it:

    • stand sideways to the direction of the pass or shot, with the puck about the middle of the blade;

    • position the blade so it is at a right angle to a line to the target;

    • try to look to where you should be passing;

    • keep the stick blade on the ice as much as you can and sweep the blade along the ice, pulling with the top hand and pushing with the bottom hand.

The forehand pass.

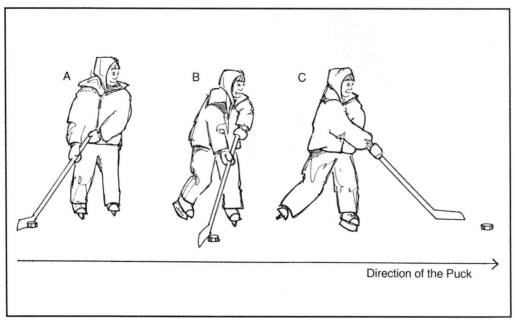

Direction of the Puck

124

Initially your body weight will be on the rear foot (A);

• as you pass the puck, transfer your weight to the front foot (B, then C);

• after you let go of the puck, let the stick follow through towards the target so that your arms, hands and stick point directly at the target.

The toe of the stick points directly at the target at the end of the follow-through. Do not lift the stick high on the follow-through, as this makes the shot less accurate and may also injure anyone who is nearby.

Stationary Backhand Passing

You will want to learn to pass from both the forehand and the backhand. The two movements are very similar. Again, in the backhand stroke the weight is shifted from the back leg to the front as the pass is made.

The stationary backhand pass.

The puck is cupped by the stick blade, and the wrists snapped or flicked (rolled inwards) at the end. Again, follow through at the end of the movement.

Backhand passes are usually shorter than the forehand, since the action is not as strong as that of the forehand. You have to practice a lot to get good.

The backhand pass should be crisp. You don't want the pass to be so hard that your partner can't pick it up, or so soft that it doesn't get to its target, or is easily intercepted.

Receiving a Pass

Receiving a pass will soon be easy, too. For receiving on both the backhand and the forehand, just remember a few key points:

• keep your stick on the ice to give your partner a target,

Receiving a pass. and keep both hands on the stick;

Allow
a little 'give'
when the puck
hits the stick

126

• try to keep the stick blade at right angles to the line you are receiving the pass along;

• as the puck hits the blade, let the stick "give" a little to cushion the impact and stop the puck from bouncing off.

Take your eyes off the puck whenever you can—you'll gradually learn to keep your head up. Keep working on it!

Following are some exercises to help practice both backhand and forehand passing—shooting and reception.

Practice the movements of passing a few times *without* a puck, and then try it with a puck or ball.

Pass to the sides of the rink from 15 feet away. Aim at a certain target, say two markers three feet apart. As you get better, move back a few feet, or make the target smaller. How many shots out of 10 can you get on target? You can make the exercise more difficult when you can consistently hit 8 out of 10, or better.

Pass to a friend and back, or even to two friends. Start at about 9 to 15 feet apart, standing still. Pass around the triangle, forehand and backhand. Go to about 30 feet apart when you get good. Can you pass right to your partner's stick so that they don't have to move it?

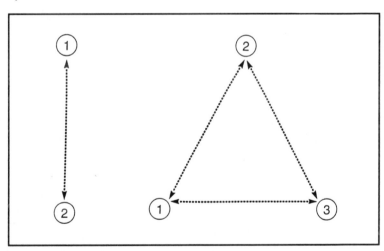

Passing around a triangle.

Pass/shoot at a target, such as an old can. See if you can move it along the ice to the far end of the rink.

Play "pig in the middle" using a puck or ball.

Leading the Skater

Once you've got good at passing to a fixed target, you can pass to a friend who is skating. Remember, you must pass to where the skater *will be* when the puck gets there.

Try to pass in front of them so that they can take the pass in stride without slowing down or speeding up. It's hard at first!

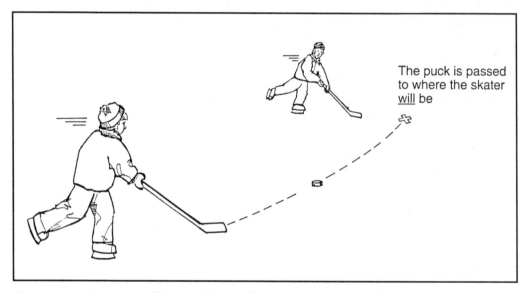

The puck is passed to where the skater <u>will</u> be

Passing and leading the skater.

Try passing at first to a partner who is skating slowly and who is about 9 feet away. How many passes out of 10 can you both complete?

If you can complete most of your passes at a certain speed and distance, then you are ready to try longer passes at a faster speed.

Get plenty of practice. Don't try to develop this skill too fast. You'll soon be able to pass accurately over a good distance.

Skating and Passing

Now you can skate with the puck, and pass to either stationary objects or moving players. Next you can work on improving your skill at passing and receiving the puck while skating.

Skate slowly at first and then speed up as you improve. On your own, skate past the boards or banks at the edge of your rink and pass the puck to the side, and then receive the puck as it bounces off the side.

Make sure you skate in both directions so you practice both your forehand and backhand. You can also pass to a friend by bouncing the puck (or ball) off the side of the rink.

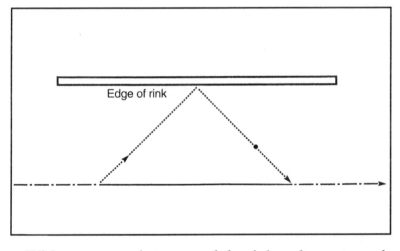

Edge of rink

Passing the puck off the boards.

With a partner, skate around the rink and pass to each other. Remember to *lead* your partner by passing in front of them as they skate along. Skate about 9 feet apart. At first skate slowly, and increase the speed as you get better. Skate and pass in both directions for forehand and backhand practice.

129

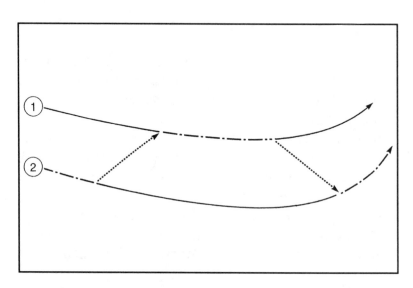

Passing to a friend.

Here are some other exercises. By now you will be able to make up your own games as well!

Forward and Backward

Forward and backward drill.

Do this in pairs:
 • A skates 30 feet with the puck and then passes to B;

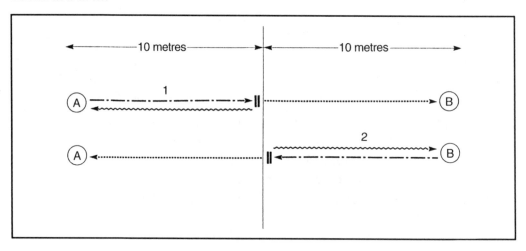

• A then stops with a two-foot stop and skates backwards to the starting position (1);
   • B then repeats the action (2).

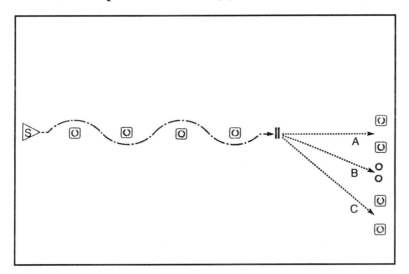

*Weaving and
shooting drills.*

Weave and Shoot

Set up markers so you can skate and
weave between them with the puck
and then shoot at a target. Try skating
both ways.
   You can make this more difficult
by:
   • increasing the distance between
yourself and the target;
   • making the target smaller;
   • passing from different angles.
When you have mastered these
skills, you will certainly be able to join
your local community league.

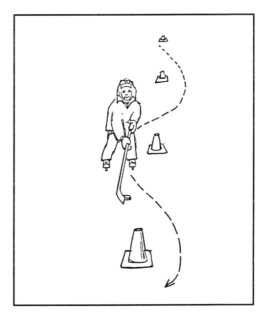

13

In–Line Skating Basics

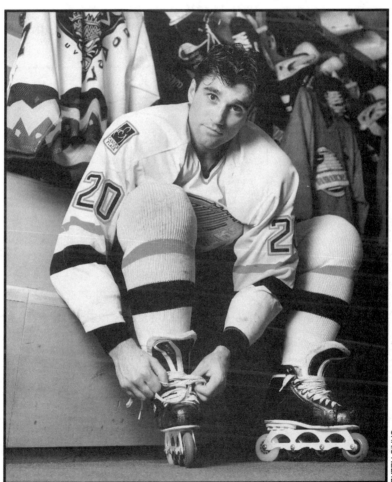

CHRIS RELKE

Many adults remember having a pair of rollerskates as a child. In the "old days" each rollerskate had a pair of wheels at the front and back.

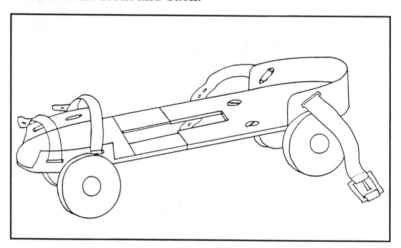

A traditional rollerskate.

Nowadays the skate craze of the past has been replaced by the "in-line" skate on which three, four or five wheels are organized in a straight line

In-line skating is also known as "Rollerblading" (named after a brand name of skate). It is fast becoming a popular sport, mainly because it is an enjoyable fitness activity that can be done in a variety of climates and locations.

Another advantage of in-line skating is that it does not involve the same stress on the ankles, knees, hips and back

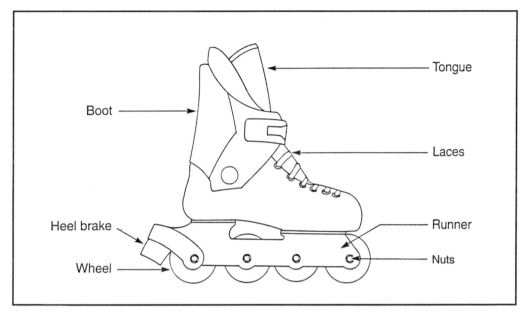

Tongue

Boot

Laces

Heel brake

Runner

Wheel

Nuts

as does running or some forms of aerobic activity, such as aerobic dance. In-line skating can be done alone, in couples, or with the entire family.

A typical in-line rollerskate.

In this chapter, we discuss the basics of selecting equipment, maintaining your in-line skate, and some safety tips for the beginning in-line skater. Later we show how some of the skills, progressions and drills described in previous chapters can be applied to learning in-line skating.

We also alert you to some critical differences between in-line skating and ice skating. Stopping while skating backwards, for example, is a more difficult skill in in-line skating than in ice skating. This is because when in-line skating you typically do not even try to stop while skating backwards, but rather you need to have developed the skill of pivoting from backwards to forward first, and then you stop while going forward!

As a result, the skill progressions described in earlier

chapters for ice skating, although similar for in-line skating, have to be approached slightly differently.

In-Line Skating and Hockey

In-line skating presents many of the same challenges as ice skating, and uses similar muscle groups. Thus, for the hockey enthusiast, in-line skating is a method by which skating-type skills and conditioning can be developed in the summer months when ice-time is rare. The puckhandling skills described earlier can also be practiced on in-line skates, and you can play roller hockey (hockey on in-line skates).

Differences between In-Line Skating and Ice Skating

Before we talk about the similarities between ice skating and in-line skating, some very important *differences* need to be mentioned. These differences are important to know because they have safety implications.

The most important difference between ice skating and in-line skating is the technique used when stopping, or trying to change direction quickly. Although ice skaters use their edges to stop and turn sharply, this is dangerous when in-line skating, as the edges of the wheels will not slide like a metal blade does on the ice.

So, if you try to stop using a hockey stop, snowplow stop or backwards T-stop wearing in-line skates, you will likely end up on your face!

It is important to remember that concrete and asphalt are less forgiving than ice. While all are hard surfaces, at least ice allows you to slide, so that some of your impact can be taken up if you fall properly. Concrete, on the other hand, produces more friction when you fall on it, so you can scrape yourself pretty badly.

Learning how to stop when using in-line skates is the single most important skill to learn. Therefore, once you feel reasonably comfortable and balanced on your in-line skates, the very first thing you need to practice is *stopping*.

Equipment and Safety

First, let's review the proper equipment you will need before you get started on your skates.

The following illustration shows what the well-dressed in-line skater is wearing this year! If fashion is not that important to you, or you want to save a little money, there are some good substitutes for the hi-tech equipment.

In-line roller-skating equipment.

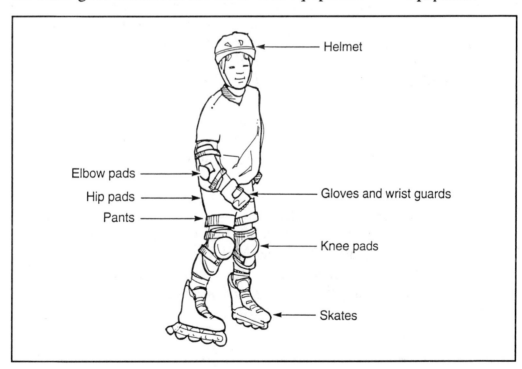

Helmet

Elbow pads

Hip pads

Pants

Gloves and wrist guards

Knee pads

Skates

137

Homemade Alternatives to In-Line Skating Equipment

Skates ....No alternative, but could be borrowed, or bought second-hand. See below about how you can make your own in-line skates out of old ice skates.

Knee Pads ....An old pair of socks cut off and padded, or volleyball knee pads.

Pants...Regular old pants, perhaps with some padding sewn into the seat and hip areas.

Elbow Pads ....If you use them for hockey you can use them for in-line skating, too.

Helmet...A bicycle helmet, or hockey helmet without the cage.

Gloves and Wrist Protectors ....An old padded pair of work or ski gloves. You can cut the ends of the fingers off to keep your hands cool if you wish. You can use some old hockey gloves too.

Making your own in-line skates

If you have an old pair of ice skates that still fit well, they can be converted to in-line skates. The wheels and wheel housing section can be purchased separately at many stores. Take these parts to a shoe repair store, have them remove the ice skate blades, and then install the in-line skates.

On the previous page we suggest some ideas for less expensive alternatives to the regular equipment. In-line skating gear, however, can also be a fashion statement, so many people may wish to buy new equipment.

As most in-line skating takes place on rough surfaces, some skin protection is advisable. Keep your skin covered if you can, especially your hips, knees, hands, wrists and elbows. These will take most of the brunt of a fall.

Selecting the Right Type of Skate

We won't get into technical details here. Your local skate store will be able to advise you about the type of skate that best fits your budget and skating goals, be they cross-training, recreation, or competition skating.

But one important tip is to "shop around" among the stores which sell in-line skates. One of our friends in the business advised us to "shop the clerk first." In other words: does the salesperson know something about in-line skates? Reading this chapter will give you some ideas about the questions to ask, and you will soon get an idea of which clerks know what they are talking about.

Different models and sizes of skates have a different number of wheels. There are also many types of in-line skates, and not all of them are suitable for the beginner. There are different types of wheels, levels of ankle/foot support, flexibility of boot, and softness or firmness of ride.

In general, the more expensive in-line skates have larger diameter wheels and more freewheeling ball bearings, which in turn produce more speed. Higher priced boots also tend to be more comfortable, better ventilated and made with better quality components.

If you are a heavier adult, you will probably want higher-priced wheels and bearings, since they are made out of harder wearing, more durable materials. This is similar to buying running shoes, where the heavier individual needs a more supportive, sturdier shoe.

Skates in the mid-price range with three or four wheels appear appropriate for beginners.

For the recreational skater, a suitable skate has:
- an easy to firm ride;
- moderate to high performance wheels;
- a normal to maximum level of foot support.

Fitting Your Skates

All adult in-line skates are based on men's sizing. Therefore, men can look for in-line skates in the same sizes as their regular shoe size.

Women should choose skates which are one-and-a-half to three sizes smaller than their usual street shoe size. So, if you are a regular size nine ladies, try a size six or seven skate.

Children's sizings fit as per shoe size.

The key to fitting your in-line skate is the *comfort fit:* your skates should feel comfortable as you wear them in the store. This is different from the moulded fit associated with ice skates, where the boot *moulds* to your foot shape with time.

The rules for choosing the correct size of in-line skates are very similar to those described for ice skates in Chapter Two:
- find a pair of skates that fits firmly and snugly around the heel, but allows you enough room to wiggle your toes. However, it is our experience that you can buy a bigger in-

line skate and get away with it. This is good for children because they can grow into a larger skate. All you need to do is to put an insert into the shoe if it is a little too large.

Make sure that your toes are not squished against the boot's toe-cap, either when your leg is straight or when your knee is bent.

Remember, you can also add an insole if the skate is too big.

If you wear prescribed orthotics, such as arch supports, they can be accomodated within most skates. Just remember to take your orthotic along with you when you are trying out sizes.

Tightly lacing or buckling the ankle area increases the ankle support.

One idea to help you find a skate that fits is to rent a pair of in-line skates similar to ones that you might buy. After trying the rental pair, take note of their size. If they feel too big try a smaller pair next time, or vice-versa.

Safety Tips

Like many fast-moving sports, in-line skating has an element of risk. Lessening the risk of injury is basically a matter of common sense. Be well-prepared, well-equipped, and take things slowly when you first get on your skates.

Remember:
• always wear your safety equipment;
• take it easy when first skating—don't go too fast too soon;
• keep away from busy streets as much as possible;
• begin skating on a level area such as an unused parking lot, school tarmac or basketball court;
• skate in uncongested areas, if possible;

- control speed when going down inclines;
- be especially courteous and careful when skating on walking or running paths. Always skate within your abilities, and be courteous to other skaters, pedestrians or other road and path users. If paths are marked, keep to your side. Check behind your shoulders before overtaking to make sure nobody is overtaking you. Tell people which side you are going to overtake them on. Always obey traffic regulations.

Some people suggest that you should not in-line skate at night. One reason for this is that you cannot see the road conditions as easily as in the day. Remember—small potholes can be big trouble.

If you choose to skate outside at night, be wise and wear reflective clothing. You might sew some reflective material on to an old jacket.

As in all sports, make sure you have an adequate supply of water when skating on hot days. This helps prevent dehydration and its effects, such as accidents due to poor concentration and fatigue. You can strap a water bottle on your back, or make sure you stop for frequent water breaks.

Many people in-line skate while wearing a portable cassette or radio with headphones. We advise against this. Although it is fun, it can lead to accidents due to concentrating on the music rather than what's going on around you, such as traffic, pedestrians and other skaters. If you must have the music, then keep the volume at a level that allows you to hear people, cyclists, other skaters and traffic approaching behind you.

Try to anticipate the road and path conditions which are coming up. That way you will be better able to handle them.

Surfaces

Avoid areas with cobblestones, gravel, water, oil, grease, sand or broken glass. These surfaces increase the chance of injury due to falling. Smooth blacktop or asphalt is best. Beginners, or those learning more complex skills such as skating downhill, should skate next to some grass, so there is a safer area on which to fall or bail out if a control problem should arise.

If you find yourself getting out of control, go for the nearest grassy area and run when you hit the grass. If you have to fall, falling forward is better than falling backward.

Maintenance of Your In-Line Skates

Like a car owner checking the safety of their tires, in-line skate owners should take care of their equipment, particularly since in-line skates have so many moving parts. Many in-line skates come with their own maintenance instructions and tools. Specific maintenance tasks include:

• checking the tightness of the axles and wheel nuts so they do not fall off while you are skating;

• checking your heel brake pads to make sure they aren't wearing out—these can easily be replaced;

• making sure that the wheels and bearings are turning freely—both wheels and bearings will need to be replaced eventually;

• follow the manufacturer's maintenance suggestions;

• rotating the wheels. In-line skate wheels need to be rotated, just like a car, depending on their wear patterns. This makes them last longer. When you notice "wheel wear" you can change your skate's wheels from front-to-back. The front wheel goes to the back and the other two move forward one position. If you find that one side of the wheel is worn more than the other you can change the wheels over to your other skate. This way the bearings are rotating the same way, but the other side of the wheel gets some wear. For more information, read the manufacturer's instructions on this, or get advice from your local store.

These are just some of the maintenance tips that will help you get the best use and most enjoyment from your in-line skates.

14

In–Line Skating Skills

First Steps: Stepping Out and Stopping

We will suggest a number of ideas for learning in-line skating. Remember also that many stores have information about in-line skating lessons, and some of these may be free.

This chapter will give you some basic skills and progressions to work from. Take care to thoroughly read this chapter before you start. You may also wish to review the sections in Chapters Four through Eleven which we think are relevant to learning in-line skating.

As we mentioned earlier, try to keep to uncrowded, quiet areas when you are first learning to skate. Empty parking lots or school grounds in the evening are great quiet places to get started. You may want to walk or drive to the practice area for your first few times.

Do not forget to put on your protective gear. Also avoid going near steep inclines before you can stop.

Here are some ideas on how to first get on your skates, take some steps, and then stop.

Your First Steps

After getting your skates on for the first time, spend a bit of time getting used to the feeling of being on wheels. Like the initial steps in learning to ice skate it can be useful to hold on to a support, such as a friend in regular shoes. This decreases your fear of falling, and encourages you to try new skills safely. Take note—another beginner on wheels is not the best support to hold on to!

If you are a parent learning to in-line skate at the same time as you are teaching your child, here are some useful tips:

• try to learn the skills yourself before you teach your child. This way you will understand what it is like to learn that skill, and you will probably give them some good learning tips. You can also be a role model to your child as to how to learn the skills.

• unless you are a very proficient skater, it is a good idea to take your own skates off while you are teaching your child. This way you can be a more stable support for them. You can also concentrate on encouraging and teaching them without worrying about your own balance.

The key tips for the beginning in-line skater are very similar to those we have suggested for the beginning ice skater. The basic stance is very similar, with bent knees which are in line with the toes of the boot. This stance will tend to keep your body weight over the front of your foot.

A useful cue is to feel as if your shin is being pressed against the tongue of the skate, just like with downhill skiing.

Another point to remember as a beginning skater is that you will tend to have a wide stance (feet wider than shoulder width apart) because it makes you feel more stable and secure. However, the wide stance does not allow you to have as much speed or control over your skates. For example, effective stopping requires that your feet are hip-width apart. So as you practice gliding try to bring your feet in so that they are hip width apart or closer.

For the first few times on the in-line skates, you might use some of the suggestions and skill progressions in previous sections of this book:

• stepping out for the first time (page 44);
• falling down and getting up (pages 46 to 48);
• gliding and gentle turns (page 52);
• sculling forward (pages 56 to 57);

- T-push and glide (pages 57 to 59).

Try some of the basic skills in a safe environment. Some readers who have ice skating skills may learn these early skills easily.

Once you have the ability to stand up, balance on your skates and take a few strides, it is time to learn how to stop.

Learning to Stop

Take the time now to slow down on your skating progress and learn how to stop.

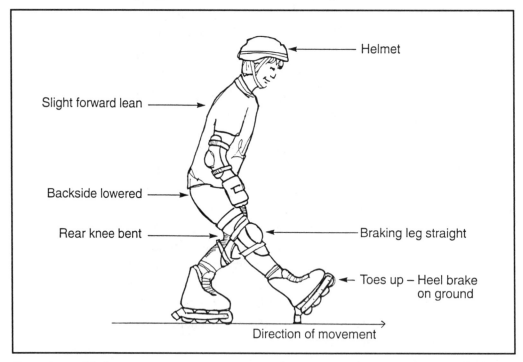

Helmet

Slight forward lean

Backside lowered

Rear knee bent

Braking leg straight

Toes up – Heel brake on ground

Direction of movement

Stopping with in-line skates.

As we have already mentioned, the technique for stopping on in-line skates is different from ice skating—*do not try to use ice skating snowplow stops when using in-line* blades. It is critical that you develop a stopping habit that is different from ice skating. Old habits are hard to break.

What happens is that experienced ice skaters quickly pick up the striding motion of in-line skating. However, they can get going too fast without having mastered the stopping skills. Similarly, once some basic skills have been mastered, beginning in-line skaters can forget, and automatically use their ice skating stops without thinking. Both of these situations can lead to accidents.

Stopping Using the Heel Brake

After you've mastered a few beginning skills try to learn how to stop using the heel brake. Most in-line skates come with a brake pad on the right boot. Some in-line skates allow you to switch the brake pad from one boot to the other. If you are not sure which foot you want to brake with, try and get a pair of skates that allow you to switch the brake pads between boots. Still other skates come with heel brakes on both skates. Some people find this to be very advantageous as they can brake with both feet; others only find that it complicates matters.

If you have a pair of skates that allows switching the brake pads over, you will have to decide which foot you want to put the brake pad on. You might want to experiment to find which foot seems more natural or effective for you.

Once you have decided on which foot you will brake with, leave the brake on that boot to develop your new stopping habit.

The best technique for stopping is to:

• raise the toes of your braking foot while pushing the foot out in front of you and pointing your toe slightly outward;

• bend your knees;

• lower your backside and lean your upper body forward—don't lean too far forward or you will topple over.

The correct stopping position is shown on page 48. To brake harder, "sit down" more and push your heel brake into the ground.

Occasionally, very rapid stops may be necessary. This can be accomplished by dragging the wheels of your rear

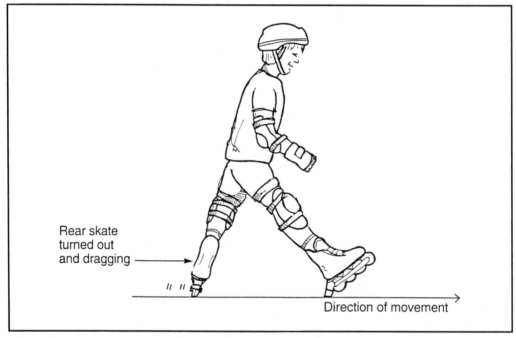

Rear skate turned out and dragging →

Direction of movement

The advanced stopping position.

skate (toes pointed out) while simultaneously using the brake pad of the leading foot.

Here are some ways to practice your stopping skills once you have learned the technique. Use the general principles for learning the skills described in Chapter Five: start slowly and use a support if necessary.

Once you have some confidence, you can increase the speed with which you perform the skill. As you master the simpler skills, move on to the more complex ones.

Take a few steps, glide, and then practice the heel-stopping technique. Remember to bring your feet apart to hip width during the glide, since effective use of your heel brake is very difficult if your feet are too wide apart. You can get the hang of the action by gliding, bending your knees, lowering your seat and touching your hands to your knees. When you wish to stop, simply straighten your braking leg.

Once you have mastered that, scull a few times to get a little more speed and then try to stop.

Do a T-push start, take two strides and then try to stop. Increase the number of strides as you become more

Practicing the stopping position.

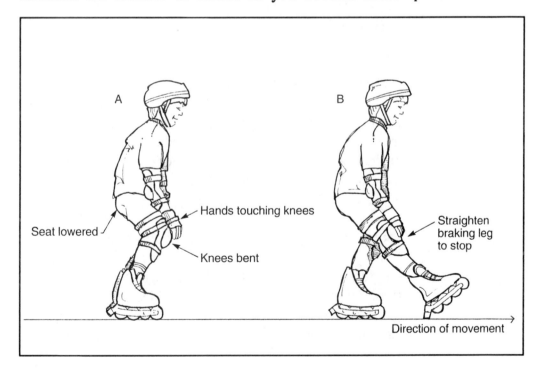

A
Seat lowered
Hands touching knees
Knees bent

B
Straighten braking leg to stop
Direction of movement

confident. Gradually increase the speed while doing this.

Try the skate-stop exercise shown on page 69 while skating in a straight line. Once you can do this, try the stopping exercises on pages 66 to 69 which involve some gliding and gentle turns.

What other exercises can you think of?

Advanced In-Line Skating Skills

Once you have developed some good stopping skills, you can go on to some more difficult in-line skating skills. We suggest you spend a fair bit of time mastering forward skating skills before getting into any pivoting or backwards skating. Again, you can refer to previous chapters on ice-skating skills, since the techniques and practice progressions are very similar.

Specific skills we would suggest you practice are:
- warming up and cooling down (page 62);
- front starts and striding (pages 72 to 75);
- edge control (pages 88 to 91);

Although this will feel different on in-line skates as compared to ice skating, the principles and mechanics are the same. Once you have developed more skill at turning on in-line skates, you should practice stopping during these skills. Then you could try:
- cross-overs (pages 91 to 95);
- emergency rapid stops. This skill has been described above. Again, this is a situation where you might slow down your progress a little. Practice these stops using the progressions suggested above for the regular in-line skating stop. For example, start with a few strides in a straight line.

Once you have mastered this, move on to practicing this stop during faster skating and then while doing turns.

Direction Changes

Once you have mastered the emergency stop technique, you can use it to help you make quick direction changes.

Practice this by doing an emergency stop, and then use your rear (dragging) skate to push you off in the direction you want, like a T-start. Your direction will be determined by where you point your front skate, and which skate you use. If you want to move to the left, point your left skate in the appropriate direction and push off with your right. Use the opposite skate if you want to move to the right.

As you get more proficient with this skill you can use it to help you change direction while you are moving fairly fast.

Pivoting

Once you have got to this stage you are doing some advanced skating skills. Again, start slowly and follow the progressions noted on pages 98 to 102.

Backward Skating

If you want to skate backwards it is best to learn how to pivot first, since braking while going backwards is difficult. You can use the heel brake, but it is not very efficient if you are skating backwards.

The backward skating section on pages 77 to 86 is just as applicable here. However, if you want to stop, it is best to execute a pivot from backward to forward and then do a normal stop.

As you get more practiced you will probably develop your own way of stopping. Also, as with most skills, you will learn new skills from other skaters as you watch them.

This is true for both adults and children.

Roller-Hockey

Hockey on in-line skates is fast becoming a popular sport. Once you have mastered in-line skating skills, you can think about playing roller-hockey using a tennis ball instead of a puck. The ball control skills are very similar to those described for puckhandling in Chapter Eleven. However, you need to be proficient at stopping and making quick turns prior to playing roller-hockey.

Try developing your skating skills without a stick so you develop a better sense of balance. Remember to keep practicing your new stopping habit with balance. When you get involved in a game you might forget your new habit, try to stop with a hockey stop, and end up on your face.

We hope that this chapter has given you some tips on how to start in-line skating, and how to learn enough basic skills to be able to play roller-hockey. Your local in-line skate store is a good resource for further information, as are some of the references cited in the final section of the book. We wish you all the best in this great sport. Happy skating!

The authors would like to acknowledge Mr. Dan Peacocke's significant contribution to the information presented in this chapter. Additional sources of information have been included in the Further Reading section.

References &
Further Reading

This book was prepared with the assistance of the following materials:

Hockey Basics

Almstedt J. (1974). *Hockey development guide* (8-18). Ottawa: Hockey Canada.

Fischler, S. & Fischler, S.W. (1983). *The Hockey Encyclopedia: the complete record of professional ice hockey.* New York: MacMillan Publishers.

Graham, T. (1977). Evaluating the youth player. *U.S. Hockey and Arena Biz,* 5, No. 7, pp. 33-35.

Kalb, J. (1977). *The easy hockey book.* Boston, MA: Houghton Mifflin Company.

Kelsey, F., Jr. (1977). Getting the young player started in hockey. *U.S. Hockey and Arena Biz,* 5, No. 9, pp. 35-36.

Lariviere, G. (1974). *Beginner's program.* Ottawa: Hockey Canada.

Lariviere, G., & Bourniva, J. (1973). *Hockey, the right start* (revised ed.) Toronto, Canada: Holt, Rinehart and Winston of Canada Ltd.

MacLean, N. (1983). *Hockey basics.* Englewood Cliffs, NJ: Prentice Hall Inc.

Myers, R. (1984). How to handle pushy parents. *Sports Now.* Vol. 2, No. 9, p. 26.

Patterson, C. & Miller, J. (1986). *C.A.H.A. model program series: Initiation program—instructors manual.* Ottawa: Government of Canada, Fitness and Amateur Sport.

Patterson, C. & Miller, J. (1986). *C.A.H.A. model program series: Initiation program—lesson manual A.* Ottawa: Government of Canada, Fitness and Amateur Sport.

Patterson, C., & Miller, J. (1986). *C.A.H.A. model program series: Initiation program— lesson manual B.* Ottawa: Government of Canada, Fitness and Amateur Sport.

Royal Canadian Air Force. (1958). *Beginning Hockey.* Ottawa, Ontario: The Queen's Printers.

Stamm, L., Fischler, S., & Friedman, R. (1977). *Power skating the hockey way.* New York: Hawthorn Books, Inc. Publishers.

Walsh, K. (1976). *Hockey for beginners.* New York: Four Winds Press.

Ice Rinks

Bloom, H. (1985). Larry Robinson moved from makeshift rinks to the top of the NHL. *Ottawa Magazine*, 5, No. 1, pp. 7, 28-33.

Gauvin, M. (1972) *Outdoor artificial rinks: Installation and maintenance*. Ottawa: CPRA.

Newfoundland and Labrador Department of Rehabilitation and Recreation, Recreation and Sports Services Division. (1976). *Outdoor rinks—ideas and suggestions*.

Rombold, C.C. (1964). *Natural ice making surfaces: A manual and survey on preparation and maintenance*. Wheeling, WV: AIPE

Tapply, R. (1976). How to construct a natural ice rink. *Park Maintenance*. 29, No. 1, pp. 6-7.

In-Line Skating

Brody, Liz (1992, October). Made in the blade: Skate your way to fitness. *Shape*, pp. 92-99, 138.

Feineman, Neil. (1992, Summer). The Essential Rollerblader. *Men's Journal*, Vol. 1, No. 1.

Lavallee, Marc. (1992, Summer). My New Sport In-line Skating. *At Your Leisure Magazine*. pp. 18, 20 & 21.

The Official Rollerblade® handbook, (1991). Rollerblade, Inc. 5101 Shady Oak Road, Minnetonka, MN 55343

Rollerblading, U of A guide.

Safe Wheel'n. Safety information and features for bicycles and in-line roller skates. Produced by United Cycle: 10344—82 Avenue, Edmonton, AB, Canada, and Alberta Cycle: 9131—118 Avenue, Edmonton, AB, Canada.

United Cycle, Edmonton. *In-line Rollerskate Rental/Demo Agreement*.

Skating Skills

Davies, V. (1983). *CANSKATE Coaches Manual*. (Anne Mason, Ed.). Canadian Figure Skating Association.

Dolan, F.E. (1974). *The complete beginner's guide to ice skating*. Garden City, New York: Doubleday and Company, Inc.

Kalb, J., & Kalb, L. (1981). *The easy ice skating book*. Boston, MA: Houghton Mifflin Company.

MacLean, N. (1984). *Ice skating basics*. Englewood Cliffs, NJ: Prentice-Hall Inc.

Stretching

Anderson, Bob. (1980). *Stretching*. Shelter Publishers.

For Those With Academic Interests...

Movement, Play, Sport and Child Development

Bloom, B.S. (1985). *Developing talent in young people*. New York: Ballantyne.

Bower, T.G.R. (1977). *The perceptual world of the child*. Cambridge, MA: Harvard University Press.

Bruner, J. (1972). The nature and uses of immaturity. *American Psychologist*, 27, pp. 687-708.

Bruner, J. (1983). *Child's Talk: Learning to use language*. Oxford, UK: Oxford University Press.

Bruner, J., Jolly, A. & Sylva, K. (Eds.) (1976). *Play: Its role in development and evolution*. Harmondsworth, U.K.: Penguin Books.

Corbin, C.B. (1980). *Textbook of motor development* (2nd Ed.). Iowa, WI: Brown.

Garvey, C. (1977) *Play: The developing child*. Cambridge, MA: Harvard University Press.

Kagan, J. (1981). *The second year: The emergence of self-awareness*, Cambridge, MA: Harvard University Press.

Kagan, J. (1984). *The nature of the child*. New York: Basic Books.

Kerr, R. (1982). *Psychomotor learning*. Toronto: Saunders College Publishing.

McClenaghan, B. & Gallahue, D. (1978). *Fundamental movement: a developmental and remedial approach*. Philadelphia, W.B. Saunders.

Oxendine, J.B. (1968). *Psychology of motor learning* (2nd ed.). Englewood Cliffs, NJ: Prentice Hall.

Singer, R. N. (Ed.) (1972). *Reading in motor learning*. Philadelphia: Lea and Febiger.

Smith, M.F.R. (1974, September/October). A preliminary case for classifying sports environments by particular objectives. *The Journal of the Canadian Association of Health, Physical Education and Recreation.*

Tanner, J.M. (1962). *Growth at Adolescence* (2nd ed.) Oxford, U.K.: Blackwell.

Tanner, J.M. (1973, September). Growing Up. *Scientific American.*

Tanner, J.M. (1978) *Fetus Into Man*. Cambridge, MA: Harvard University Press.

Wickstrom, R.L. (1970). *Fundamental motor patterns*. Philadelphia: Lea and Febiger.

Yawkey, T.D. & Pellegrini, A.D. (Eds.) (1984). *Child's play: Developmental and applied*. Hillsdale, NJ: Lawrence Erlbaum Associates.

HOCKEY BOOKS FROM POLESTAR PRESS

Polestar Press publishes some of Canada's best-selling hockey titles. These books are available in your local bookstore, or directly from Polestar Press. Please send a cheque for the retail price of the book, plus the relevant shipping and handling costs: $4.00 for shipping the first book in your order, and $1.00 for each subsequent book. American customers may pay in U.S. funds.

All-New Allstar Hockey Activity Book • *Noah Ross & Julian Ross* • $6.95 Can/$6.95 US • A new collection of quizzes, games, radical stats and trivia for young hockey fans.

Allstar Hockey Activity Book • *Noah Ross & Julian Ross* • $6.95 Can/$6.95 US • Hockey history, Soviet hockey cards, and hours of hands-on fun for young hockey fans.

Basic Hockey And Skating Skills: The Backyard Rink Approach • *Jeremy Rose & Murray Smith* • $16.95 Can/$14.95 US • A comprehensive, non-competitive method for learning the fundamentals of ice and in-line skating. Also includes plans for building a backyard rink.

Behind The Mask: The Ian Young Goaltending Method, Book One • *Ian Young & Chris Gudgeon* • $18.95 Can/$16.95 US • Drills, practice techniques, equipment considerations and more are part of this unique goaltending guide.

Beyond The Mask: The Ian Young Goaltending Method, Book Two • *Ian Young & Chris Gudgeon* • $18.95 Can/$16.95 US • Book Two of this effective goaltending series focuses on intermediate goalies and their coaches.

Countdown to the Stanley Cup: An Illustrated History of the Calgary Flames • *Bob Mummery* • $19.95 Can/$17.95 US • Highlights of nine exciting seasons of this successful hockey club.

Country On Ice • *Doug Beardsley* • $9.95 Can/$8.95 US • The story of Canada's compelling attraction to the game of hockey.

Elston: Back To The Drawing Board • *Dave Elston* • $12.95 Can/$11.95 US • Sports-cartoonist Elston's comic view of the world of hockey.

Elston's Hat Trick • *Dave Elston* • $14.95 Can/$12.95 US • The third in this best-selling cartoonist's collection of irreverent, hilarious hockey cartoons.

Fuhr On Goaltending • *Grant Fuhr & Bob Mummery* • $16.95 Can/$14.95 US • The ultimate guide to goaltending from the ultimate goalie.

Hockey's Young Superstars • *Eric Dwyer* • $16.95 Can/$14.95 US • Profiles and action photos of Bure, Jagr, Lindros, Mogilny, Sakic, Modano and others.

The Rocket, The Flower, The Hammer and Me: An All-Star Collection of Canadian Hockey Fiction • *Doug Beardsley*, editor • $9.95 Can/$8.95 US • Exciting stories from writers like W.P. Kinsella, Hugh MacLennan, Brian Fawcett and others.

Order books from:
Polestar Press Ltd., 1011 Commercial Drive, 2nd Floor, Vancouver, BC, Canada, V5L 3X1